T0320650

Change Management for Risk Professionals

Change Management for Risk Professionals

James J. Leflar, Jr

CRC Press
Taylor & Francis Group
Boca Raton London New York

CRC Press is an imprint of the
Taylor & Francis Group, an **informa** business

First edition published 2021
by CRC Press
2 Park Square, Milton Park, Abingdon, Oxon, OX14 4RN

and by CRC Press
6000 Broken Sound Parkway NW, Suite 300, Boca Raton, FL 33487-2742

© James J. Leflar, Jr.

CRC Press is an imprint of Informa UK Limited

British Library Cataloguing-in-Publication Data
A catalogue record for this book is available from the British Library

---

Library of Congress Cataloging-in-Publication Data

Names: Leflar, James J., author.
Title: Change management for risk professionals /
James J. Leflar, Jr.
Description: First edition. | Boca Raton : CRC Press, 2021.
| Includes
   bibliographical references and index.
Identifiers: LCCN 2020042123 (print) | LCCN 2020042124
(ebook) | ISBN 9780367251598 (hardback) |
ISBN 9780367711382 (paperback) | ISBN 9780429318573 (ebook)
Subjects: LCSH: Organizational change--Management. |
Risk management.
Classification: LCC HD58.8 .L425 2021 (print) | LCC
HD58.8 (ebook) | DDC 658.4/06--dc23
LC record available at https://lccn.loc.gov/2020042123
LC ebook record available at https://lccn.loc.
gov/2020042124

ISBN: 978-0-367-25159-8 (hbk)
ISBN: 978-0-367-71138-2 (pbk)
ISBN: 978-0-429-31857-3 (ebk)

Typeset in Palantino
by SPi Global, India

I dedicate this book to the change practitioners working as risk professionals and all those risk professionals who will become change practitioners.

CONTENTS

Part I

Part 2

Part 3

Appendix A

Appendix B

Appendix C

Appendix D

LIST OF FIGURES

PREFACE

Change happens! Perhaps a better way to say that worn-out phrase is that change must happen! Organizations are dynamic and reflect the surrounding environment. Consider personal computers and associated devices; the change consequences from these items are considerable. Organizations exist within a complex and changing environment. The changes within the organizational context (e.g., societal, technological, and customer preferences) place pressure upon the organization to remain relevant and competitive. Change is not inherently wrong; our perceptions of the change make it negative or positive. A perceived negative change can become a real opportunity for improvement if desired. Systemic degradation and irrelevancy are the results of an organization that fails to acknowledge the reality of change. For instance, the traditional retail brick and mortar store is facing the dominance of Amazon as a customer convenience. The discussion so far has focused on strategic issues that are critical and meaningful to organizations. Still, the focus of this book is more practical and targets risk practitioners seeking more information about change management. Yes, tactical issues are also critical and meaningful to organizations, but often get lost in the everyday project-oriented tasks of a typical day.

The purpose of this book is to provide a practical discussion about change management for risk practitioners. There is a real need for an uncomplicated text that helps educate non-change management professionals involved in risk-oriented change initiatives. A risk professional or practitioner is a description of a group of people that focus on addressing risk-oriented issues. The risk professionals discussed in the book are from the professional disciplines of security (physical and IT), business continuity, disaster recovery, crisis management, emergency management, risk management, organizational resilience management, and other protective activities. While specific subjects are identified, the information contained in the book is of value to anyone involved in change initiatives. Everyone in an organization should be considered a risk practitioner. The IT profession is familiar with change management because of the need to manage the complexity of additions of hardware, software, and processes into the network environment. While IT professionals may be familiar with the basics of change management, they can also benefit from the discussion in this book because the real focus of change is the process involving people. Considerable resources (e.g., time, money, support, and reputations) are used to develop and implement projects and programs only to fail because of a lack of understanding of the complexities of change management. Enhancing the understanding of change for risk professionals is the goal of the book.

WHY RISK PROFESSIONALS

The personal justification to author a change management text for risk professionals came after years of experience as a risk professional and specializing as organizational resilience thought leader. One of the foundations of organizational resilience is change management at all levels of the organization. Practitioners often focus on the implementation of the project and the accomplishment of the goals but fail to consider the change dynamics involved in the project adequately. Anecdotal evidence and requests from several risk professionals was enough reason to author the book. The intended audience of this book is in every organization with disciplines that focus on the development and implementation of risk-oriented initiatives. That is a rather widespread audience, but that is because change management affects every aspect of an organization.

The alignment of change initiatives with organizational goals is a recommended management approach. It will contribute to the enhancement of the bottom line. The alignment of all projects and programs with organizational strategic goals is just good business. The expense of organizational resources should benefit the organization in some way to justify the use. The use of the phrase organizational development (OD) professional is occasionally used to describe a person with advanced knowledge and skills in the field of change management. With the right education and training, anyone can become an OD professional, but it requires advanced knowledge. Likewise, the use of **change agent** appears throughout the book. A change agent is anyone that seeks to transform an organization or group through persistence and personable skill techniques resulting in a positive outcome (i.e., change) that is in line with the desired goals. The change manager and change champion are examples of a change agent. However, there is a possibility that a low-level worker with the knowledge and gravitas associated with a change could be a change agent.

ACKNOWLEDGEMENTS

I started my doctoral studies in early January 2015 (25 years after completing my Master of Arts degree in criminal justice at Temple University) at Colorado Technical University, completing my management doctorate in the middle of December 2017. While I was focused on my specialty, organizational resilience, my actual concentration was in organizational development and change. It is a foundational component of organizational resilience. For 3 full years, I worked every day to enhance my academic skills, and I received endless support and encouragement from my colleagues and professors. I owe my fellow cohort 50 doctoral students and my professors a heartfelt and sincere thank you; I learned a great deal from you, and I miss the regular discussions.

I also thank my colleagues (i.e., Edward McCormack, Mark Kern, CBCP, Harvin Perez, CBCP, Rajvir Singh, John Kelly, and Patrick R. Highsmith) at Booz Allen Hamilton for providing an environment that embraces change as an integral component of the organization. Their involvement and support of a significant change initiative have provided numerous ideas for this book. While I did not use any proprietary Booz Allen information, situations occurred that reminded me of various critical considerations when initiating change.

AUTHOR

Dr. James J. Leflar, Jr, DM, CPP, MBCP
Dr. Leflar holds a master's degree in criminal justice and a doctorate in management with a concentration in organizational development and change. He holds board certifications through ASIS International as a Certified Protection Professional (CPP) – advanced security management, and through the Disaster Recovery Institute International, Master Business Continuity Professional (MBCP) – master's level advanced certification in business continuity.

Dr. Leflar is an active delegate to the U.S. Technical Advisory Group, ISO TC 292, for Security and Resilience. He is also a member and former chair of the ASIS International Crisis Management and Business Continuity Council. Dr. Leflar is a subject matter expert for Booz Allen Hamilton's Business Continuity Program Office and an adjunct professor at Saint Leo University, teaching criminal justice and public safety courses.

As a thought leader of organizational resilience, Dr. Leflar has authored numerous documents on risk to include his co-authored book *Organizational Resilience: Managing the Risks of Disruptive Events – A Practitioner's Guide.* His research interests focus on organizational resilience, business continuity, risk management, crisis management, and change management.

ORGANIZATION OF THE BOOK

Change Management for Risk Professionals consists of three sections (i.e., grouped chapters) and several examples in the appendices. Part one (i.e., Chapters 1–3) establishes the foundation of change management for risk professionals, conceptual frameworks of change management, and various issues concerning change. The established foundation provides the reader with the necessary understanding to proceed with more complex issues surrounding change management. Special attention is given to the resistance to change and change initiative failures.

Part two (i.e., Chapters 4 and 5) addresses the conceptual dynamics between leaders and managers. Are leaders and managers the same, or is there a difference? There is an extensive discussion about leadership types and approaches, and the concept of a change practitioner. Chapter 5 focuses on a variety of theoretical issues and attempts to position change management within the organization.

The final section is part three, consisting of Chapters 6 and 7. Several essential topics appear in the section, such as maintaining the change and preparing for the next change initiative. It is vital to maintain the change momentum resulting in the institutionalization of the change initiative. There is an industry case study as an example of the change practitioner to consider. Chapter 7 provides final thoughts on lifelong learning and the importance of inculcating change into both the organizational culture and change manager's philosophy on the concept of change. Change is not necessarily adverse; how change is used and interpreted is the defining issue.

At the end of each chapter, there are at least two exercises designed to elaborate on the concepts discussed in that chapter. The activities are opportunities to think about the ideas and issues surrounding change initiatives. The appendices consist of templates and forms to help the novice change manager develop a change project.

Part 1

1

Change Management

No man ever steps in the same river twice, for it's not the same river and he's not the same man.

Heraclitus, Greek philosopher

LEARNING OBJECTIVES

The learning objectives of this chapter are:

- The Concept of Change Management
- A Systems Perspective and Change
- Kotter's Change Model

THE CONCEPT OF CHANGE MANAGEMENT

Change management is much more than maintaining control over the changes to a project. Many people might consider that the extent of change management, but that is a limited and inadequate view of the power of change management. Change management is about how to plan, facilitate, empower, and achieve a desired state of change within an organization. Change management involves as much work as the actual change initiative (i.e., project).

While the achievement of a change initiative will, or at least should, contribute to the enhancement of organizational goals and the bottom line, change management is a more complex concept than it appears. Change is a process of moving from a current state of existence to a new state of existence. Lewin (1951) described the change theory in his classic model of unfreezing–changing–refreezing. The model expresses a behavioral evaluation of a situation that allows for the desire to change, the actual change, and the willingness to accept the new state (Lewin, 1951). Lewin's model is the foundation of change theory. However, the complexity of change is perhaps best described in Kruger's (1996) iceberg model.

Figure 1.1 is adapted from Kruger's (1996) model and presents a visual depiction of Kruger's (1996) diagram. The iceberg model of change describes the apparent aspects of change implementation, such as project scope components, allotted project time, and project cost – these are the visible portions of the iceberg (Kruger, 1996).

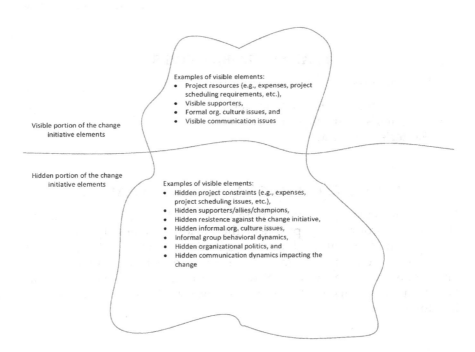

Figure 1.1 Change Management Iceberg Model - Adapted from Kruger (1996).

The exciting part of the Kruger (1996) model is the portion hidden beneath the visible surface, such as communication dynamics, resistance to change, the perceptions of those involved in the change, hidden supporters and opponents to the change, and the involvement of leadership. It is common for managers involved in a change initiative to focus on the visible implementation issues because those issues result from practical project experience. However, ignoring or failing to recognize the hidden aspects of the project will doom the initiative to failure.

Decker et al. (2012) examined the implementation failure rate of projects and concluded that while studies have indicated dubious rates as high as 93% and as low as 28%, the failure rate is likely between 50% to approximately 70%. Hughes (2011) indicated that there is no empirical data to support the popular claim of 70% initiative failure. The association between a poor understanding of the "hidden" elements noted in Kruger's iceberg model, the lack of a systems perspective throughout the change initiative, and a partial or complete disregard of Kotter's 8-step model (1996, 2012) ensure the failure of the intended change. Conversely, there is a higher chance of success if a change practitioner applies the concepts of change management, Kotter's change model, and reliable project management techniques to any change initiative. Failure of many projects is associated with a lack of understanding of the nature and dynamics of organizational systems. Organizations are complex systems, and a change initiative must become part of the organization through an acceptance of a systems perspective.

SYSTEMS AND CHANGE

Since organizations consist of systems, it is essential to understand the nature and complexity of a system. An organizational system consists of the formal and informal structure (e.g., an organizational chart and working relationships), the processes that constitute the work of the organization (e.g., the internal and external interdependent activities), and the culture of the organization (e.g., the interrelated internal and external interdependencies of the people). Busby (2017) indicated rightly that any change initiative is inextricably connected with the culture of the organization.

Change is about working to involve people in making changes in an organization and in their behaviors to the extent of the change. For instance, consider a security project involving the implementation of photo ID cards and the use of the cards to enter a facility. The security department expects everyone to show their ID card upon entry to a building. However, the employees never had to show their IDs before. It is essential to realize the influence the change initiative will have on the organizational culture, and the influence the culture will have on the change initiative (Busby, 2017).

The organizational system always operates and may have a hidden influence on the outcome of a change initiative. An organizational system has interrelated and interdependent processes that work together to achieve organizational goals. One process might require inputs from another function and produces an output that is used by another process; the more complex the organization, the more complex the system.

Figure 1.2 illustrates a high-level perspective of a fundamental organizational system. The board of directors interacts with senior leadership to develop the high-level goals that impact the industry and the strategic

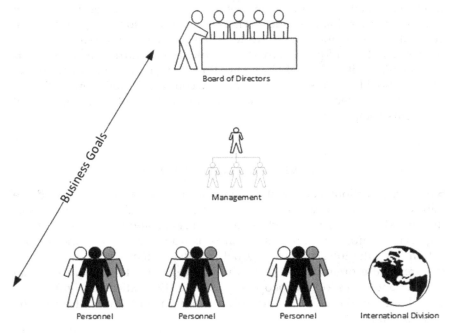

Figure 1.2 High-Level Organizational Systems Perspective.

vision of the organization. Senior leadership works with middle management to develop achievable business goals to facilitate the achievement of the market goals of the organization. The middle managers work with the employees to establish the enabling goals to promote the business unit goals that facilitate the high-level organizational goals. Each level of the organization is interrelated and interdependent upon the other levels. In addition to domestic business relations, the organization must include any international business considerations. An effective organization will ensure that all levels of the organization, along with the various major components, work together well to achieve the business goals.

Since an organization does not operate within a vacuum (i.e., the internal environment), the external environment is a critical component of the systems perspective of the organization. Figure 1.3 provides a basic

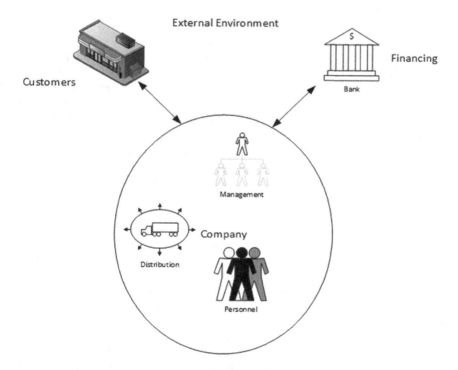

Figure 1.3 Business Relationship with External Environment.

view of the relationship between the internal or company environment and the external environment involving the customers and any necessary financing for the company. For instance, the company develops plans and goals to achieve a product(s) that will interest the customers. The company borrows money from various financing sources to allow the company to operate and produce the desired outcome. The product is created and distributed to the stores or outlets that would enable the customers to purchase the product. Public opinion and external regulators also interact with the organization influencing the viability of the product. The external environment has a significant impact on any product that a company offers to the public. The cycle continues as new goals and products are developed and sold.

While the business relationship of the internal and external systems indicated in Figure 1.3 highlights the prominent business system, Figure 1.4 focuses on the internal organizational system that makes the organization function. Figure 1.4 does reflect all the possible departments in an organization; the figure is illustrative for the discussion.

Risk professionals must understand the internal systemic perspective. Each department presented in Figure 1.4 interacts with the other departments exchanging inputs and outputs to create and achieve various goals throughout the organization. Each business unit is dependent upon other business units to operate. For instance, marketing promotes a product that the sales team sells to customers. The manufacturing department creates the product, and quality assurance verifies the quality. Packaging ensures the product is packaged safely based on feedback from customer service. The finance and legal departments perform critical roles to ensure success. At the same time, IT and telecom provide the infrastructure so that the employees can perform their respective jobs.

The supplier icon represents the supply chain system, which is often as complex, and sometimes more so than the organization's complexity. All of the departments and processes function as part of the system to ensure the organization achieves the functional and strategic goals – this is an excellent example of synergy; the sum of the system is more significant than any single process.

Several teams are not reflected in Figure 1.4 but play critical roles in the success of the entire system, the risk professionals. Security, risk management, business continuity (BC), disaster recovery, and facilities

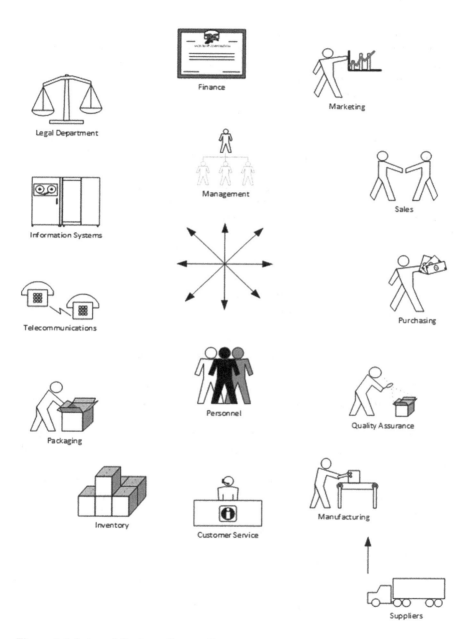

Figure 1.4 Internal Systems Perspective.

management are some of the examples that allow the business operation to function with the necessary protective measures to safeguard the people and the property assets of the organization. The risk professionals must understand the organizational systems that operate and the impact that change might have on the system. A change initiative designed to affect a single process within a department might have considerable influence on another process in a different department.

A change initiative proposed by the security department intended to mitigate the risk of release associated with personally identifiable information of customers (e.g., financial applications for a car) could have unforeseen negative consequences. For instance, the security team installs a series of new security cameras covering an area where loans are processed. The security team failed to provide proper notification beyond the processing team leadership. The employees see the latest cameras and believe their respective managers are watching them for work productivity and break documentation. The cameras were intended to increase security, but instead created a labor relations issue because the initiative was not appropriately communicated; one business unit created problems for another business unit(s) because of poor change management practices.

Another example of a negative impact involves the new technician in a small IT department making changes to the accessibility of programs (i.e., limited permissions to an application, thereby removing access to the program for some people) without notifying everyone using the programs. While the action could have been a mistake or an oversight by the new employee, the result has systemic implications within the organization. Change the example to an email server interacting with the active directory; the change could result in hundreds of people not having email access (Figure 1.4).

Figure 1.5 illustrates the external interdependencies and interrelatedness of organizations. The high-rise building in the center represents an organization with connections to the surrounding business. The surrounding companies provide food, dry cleaning services, transportation, office supplies, and many other resources upon which the central organization depends. The surrounding businesses rely on vendor relationships as indicated by the arrows (i.e., Figure 1.5) – it is a societal dependencies system. The example depicted in Figure 1.5 is appropriate at the local, regional, state, country, and international levels.

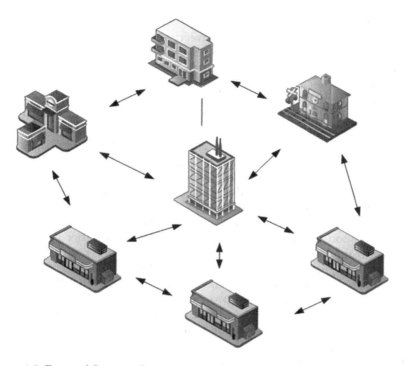

Figure 1.5 External Systems Perspective – The Influence of Societal Involvement.

SITUATIONAL EXAMPLE: BUSINESS CONTINUITY AND A SYSTEMS PERSPECTIVE

For instance, the hypothetical business ABZ Corp. is a mid-sized manufacturer of the Widget Weasel. The product is produced in Pennsylvania and is the primary profit source for the company. The workforce consists of management and non-unionized production units. ABZ is attempting to break into other markets as a diversification approach within the strategic plan. As part of the organizational review, the CEO has requested a review and update on the protective measures (risk protections) within the organization; they are concerned about the organization's ability to withstand a severe business interruption.

The BC team is part of the risk management department. Ten BC professionals are developing a new BC program (BCP) for the organization.

The former continuity director used approaches that he learned over many years, and most of the plans and recovery documents were still in binders on shelves. The new BC director, Sally, was hired with a mandate to modernize the program. Sally is a champion of change initiatives within organizations to foster transformative change.

Sally began her new job by establishing her presence in the organization; she met with a variety of mid-level managers. She wanted to create both a professional and personal relationship with these leaders. The BC director asked many questions and listened to the answers, ensuring that the managers knew she was there to help safeguard the business operation and people of the organization. Sally also made sure that the managers understood that she valued their involvement – they were critical to the success of the business continuity program.

Sally took a systems perspective when looking at the organization. She understood that each process was interrelated to other processes in the organization. Most processes had upstream and downstream dependencies throughout the organization. Figure 1.6 depicts the relationship dependencies between a single process (i.e., HR Generalist Process) and the upstream and downstream processes. The upstream processes have information or perform a function (i.e., produce output) that is necessary for the HR Generalist Process to operate appropriately. The downstream processes require information or output from the HR Generalist Process to function. In a system, each process is related to other processes and is required for the entire organization to function as leadership expects.

There is an important reality to remember when considering the parts of a system. There are formal processes that relate to documented dependency mapping and organizational charts, and there are informal relationships between people. The informal relationships create additional

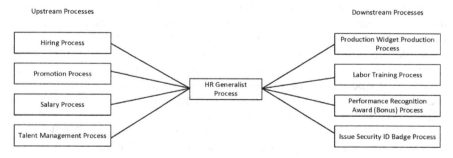

Figure 1.6 Process Dependency Mapping – Systems Perspective.

systems dependencies that are outside of the officially recognized processes. For instance, if there is a long-term employee of the organization with extensive institutional knowledge, the person may act as an unofficial resource to accomplish goals or functions – "go ask Joe, he knows how to get that done without the red tape." Unofficial resources often circumvent formal processes to facilitate the completion of a task or function; the relationships are interpersonal friendships.

COVID-19 SYSTEMS EXAMPLE

The spread and impact of the COVID-19 virus (2019–2021) is an example of the devastating implications on societal systems. The virus spread throughout the world via mass transit systems across the globe. Taking a flight from Asia to Europe or the United States to Europe is relatively fast. Within hours, a person carrying the virus can begin spreading the disease thousands of miles away without showing any signs of infection. The population of numerous countries became infected through routine travel and community interaction.

The global society is an extensive system with a large number of interdependencies, including travel, supply chain distribution, medical services, food, household needs, entertainment, and education. Consider the relationship between parents, jobs, social distancing, closed businesses and schools, and the supervision of children during COVID-19. While many parents with corporate jobs telework, there is a large portion of the United States workforce unable to telework and must suffer layoffs. There is the issue of some parents in essential positions like nurses, doctors, and food service industry workers (e.g., fast food and grocery stores); those workers holding jobs that required them to go to work while their children are home were forced to make difficult decisions. With the daycare and schools closed, those workers had to make decisions about the safety of their children from the pandemic and a supervision perspective.

Extended families living together had the added dynamic of elderly family members exposed to workers going in and out of the household. Many impoverished families holding jobs that require attendance are unable to stay at home to supervise children. Elderly family members might not have the ability to babysit because of the dangers of the pandemic. The complex system of the functional family is critical to the broader societal issues like the economy, the education system, and societal health.

While the spread within a community impacted families, there was also an impact on the economy and numerous businesses. People became ill and stayed home or went into the hospital resulting in manufacturing to decline. Orders for subcomponent products remained unfulfilled. Without products to deliver, transport companies faltered. Without critical components, larger products such as cell phones and computers remained unfinished, and customers were waiting for new products. Since Asian countries are key supply centers for technology components, when the populations of China, South Korea, Taiwan, and Japan became infected and unable to work, industries closed down. The closure of these manufacturing centers had drastic impacts on numerous other technology manufacturers. Systems are made up of numerous interdependencies and interrelated processes. If there is an impact on sections of the system, the ripple will be felt throughout the system.

KOTTER'S CHANGE MODEL

Organizing and explaining the proposed change process is best explained by Dr. John Kotter's 8-step change model (Kotter, 1996, 2012). The 8-step model is an excellent approach to understanding and achieving change initiatives. The strength of Kotter's model is the practical value it provides in viewing comprehensive change management initiatives. The eight components of Kotter's model (Kotter, 1996, 2012) are:

- Justification
- Establishing Support
- Establishing a Connection between the Initiative and the Employees
- Effective Communication
- Managing Resistance to Change
- Practical Plans
- Momentum through Communication
- Institutionalization of the Initiative

JUSTIFICATION OF THE CHANGE INITIATIVE

The justification of the change initiative as a legitimate organizational project is essential for both political and cultural reasons within the organization. The use of organizational resources must be aligned with established goals, thereby gaining management approval to proceed. Management approval enhances the likelihood that organizational employees will support the change initiative. Once management orders a project to begin, it will happen, won't it? Well, the project may begin, but that does not mean everyone will support the plan. There is more to gaining support than expectations.

Establishing personal and team milestones are necessary for the effective management of the program resulting in timely planning and implementation. The success of the BCP is the establishment and maintenance of an active image designed to protect the people and the organization. Promoting an active BC image based on accurate, fact-based information, and genuine interest in the employees wins critical support and demonstrates our concern for their best interests. A critical communication issue is the inclusion of actual and dramatic examples that demonstrate the direct value of the BCP to the organization – working together; we make a difference.

SUPPORT INVOLVES MAKING ALLIES AND FINDING CHAMPIONS

Organizational projects involve teamwork and developing influential allies to support the project throughout the organization. Approved projects do not always survive the perils of organizational infighting and empire building. Budgets are often tight, and clear justifications associated with clear management support are necessary for the advancement of the initiative. The process of making allies takes time and involves meeting people, demonstrating a commitment to an alliance, honesty, and non-threatening overtures. There are people in every organization that feel threatened by peers and subordinates; they are insecure in their abilities. Gaining their support might rest on making them feel secure and valued as a partner in the change initiative. Making allies and gaining support from others will take time; it is a daily goal to achieve – be patient.

RELATE THE INITIATIVE TO THE EMPLOYEES – CREATE VESTED INTERESTS

Engaging the organization to participate in risk-related activities is challenging, but achievable if the employees understand the issues. The project manager must capture the interest of the employees and engage them in developing the desired outcome (e.g., a world-class business continuity program). Marketing is a powerful tool to "sell" the project/program. The regular and constant marketing of the program and the associated activities ensure people remember the importance of the program.

The employees will learn about the initiative through the program's vision statement, mission statement, and program values. The inclusion of the vision statement, mission statement, and values on the program intranet site demonstrates the seriousness and commitment of the company risk-related initiative. For instance,

> **Vision Statement:** Facilitate corporate resilience at Trivia Nerds, LLC, with comprehensive business continuity planning, preparedness activities, and employee engagement.
> **Mission Statement:** Through a comprehensive and collaborative business continuity program consisting of corporate continuity plans, effective recovery strategies, a training and exercise program, and continuous improvement, Trivia Nerds, LLC, is dedicated to ensuring the resilience of personnel and business operations.
> **BCP Values:**
>
> * Embrace the Trivia Nerds, LLC values as primary tenants of the Resilience Office;
> * Acknowledge the complexity of the organizational system at Trivia Nerds, LLC and incorporate that knowledge into the BC program;
> * Promote iterative, continuous improvement of the BC program;
> * Promote a collegial, collaborative, and silo-free organizational environment dedicated to developing strong preparedness-oriented relationships.

The above examples focus on business continuity, but adjustments in the text will provide similar examples for disaster recovery, security, crisis management, facilities management, and other risk-oriented professions. The intent is to present a sincere and authentic message to the company employees showing concern for the well-being of the company and the employees.

COMMUNICATION

A critical element in creating transformative change is gaining the active support of the people involved in the change through effective communication. The process of sending a message to an audience and ensuring that the message is understood is the responsibility of the sender. If the audience does not understand the message, the effort has failed because the sender did not craft an understandable message. Avoid long, information-packed email messages as a format. It is more effective to break a long message into two or three smaller messages as part of a series of educational briefs. A WebEx or Team video/audio message is an excellent approach to reach a socially remote workforce. Make the message simple, clear, genuine, and personal; get the audience to believe in the message as something relevant to the listener.

The change manager wants employees to understand and embrace the value of initiative on a personal level. Sharing the success of the project/program with those involved is necessary for honest engagement. All information must come from accurate and fact-based sources. The use of examples (i.e., stories) will help create the initiative story at the company. Stories are more accessible for people to remember and relate to when learning something new. An essential communication consideration is the need to send a message that is understood; use plain, non-jargon language that everyone will understand. The story will allow people to relate to the message on a personal level – that hooks people into believing the message.

ADDRESS RESISTANCE TO CHANGE

The empowerment of the workforce is critical to successful change. Promote involvement, creativity, seek ideas (i.e., comments and feedback) from the employees, and recognize achievements. Effective change is attributable to the employees, not the managers. Managers provide the resources, structure, and guidance throughout the change initiative. However, the employees must willingly participate in the change to see success. For instance, recognize business units for achieving milestones such as business impact analysis (BIA) completion or exercise participation.

Recognize the feedback from employees that help improve the change initiative. Feedback is a great way to build the involvement of employees and show that they are essential to the success of the project/ program. The manager should spread the credit for success – the manager is not the key component for success; the employees are the linchpin for success.

DEVELOP THE IMPLEMENTATION PLAN TO CAPTURE REGULAR LOW-HANGING FRUIT (PLANNED WINS)

Creating short-term wins (i.e., often referred to as low-hanging fruit) provides the change initiative with feedback from users and management, allows for the recognition of participants, engenders belief in the change initiative, and reduces the power of anyone negatively criticizing the change. Maintaining the morale of the participants and reenergizing the change effort is critical to the overall momentum of the project. Think about a typical change project and the cycles of activity that occur. The short-term wins help to motivate people and propel the project forward.

Communicating the project's accomplishments is a great way to maintain awareness and the success of the initiative. The successes that are expected (low-hanging fruit) should appear in the communication and change plans. Planning to achieve helps ensure the success, and listing a planned accomplishment in the communication plan facilitates the message strategy of regular, pertinent updates.

REINFORCE THE INITIATIVE WITH REGULAR COMMUNICATIONS – KEEP THE ENERGY GOING

Maintaining a sense of urgency and flow of activities keeps the work progressing. Maintaining the momentum of the project is essential through to completion – avoid the endless issue Sisyphus faced with the boulder. Plan for the continuation of the initiative and the reenergizing of the people and the activities. Keep a steady flow of energy going into the initiative so that the activities maintain forward momentum.

Regular updates to management and the organization show professionalism and keep the change initiative in the eyes of the participants. It is wise to have a communication strategy that is grounded in a marketing approach.

PROJECT CHANGE TO A PROGRAM – MAKE IT PART OF THE ORGANIZATIONAL CULTURE

Moving the project to a program status creates the expectation that maintenance of the program is necessary to keep the work progressing. Regular updates on the program and "keeping the program in everyone's face" is necessary to avoid people forgetting about the accomplishments. A useful way to view the change process is a cycle of movement from planning through evaluation with iterative change and continuous improvement as the constants.

Examples of Action Items for a Business Continuity Change Initiative

These action items will facilitate the business continuity change initiative:

- Gain senior leadership support of a governance charter to proceed;
- Identify a senior-level champion for the business continuity program;
- Partner with change management professionals at the company to facilitate the change initiative;
- Prepare messages for management supporting the business continuity program and encouraging the involvement of the company employees, especially managers;
- Begin developing a communication strategy – multiple approaches for a diverse audience, fact-based and honest examples demonstrating our concern for the employees and the business – the constant marketing of the program is vital;
- Develop a company intranet page to promote the development and ongoing activities of the initiative – list the vision statement, mission statement, and values;
- Use a message mapping approach to convey business continuity to a general audience;
- Communicate the business continuity program support to the affected audience;
- A clear message of the benefits of the initiative for the individual company employee, as well as the organization;
- Establish manager, associate, and team milestones (e.g., training, crisis plan exercising, business impact analysis completion/updates, and revision efforts) associated with business continuity;
- Engage the business continuity coordinators as active participants in the process, and make them active participants – share the success of the program with them;

19

- Continue to promote BC data tool as self-serve to engage employees in business continuity activities;
- Promote involvement and recognize achievements;
- Review training to ensure it is current, fact-based, understandable, and delivered in different approaches (e.g., lecture for small groups, online as a self-serve multimedia lesson, and online documents as reference guides;
- Make business continuity a local team and manager responsibility to generate interest, which translates into action (i.e., involve audit and provide regular updates on business continuity program progress to management);
- Develop a continuous improvement component into the program to ensure ongoing updates;
- Develop a comprehensive strategy and long-term plan for a future change initiative organization with proper staffing levels and professional competence (if applicable). Consider using established approaches or standards to maintain momentum and the importance of the program. Not all standards are appropriate for every organization or location; focus on the best options for the organization.

An excellent way to think about change management within an organization is to place yourself on the receiving end of a change initiative. Treat the organizational audience as you would want to be treated. Provide meaningful information before the change to build support and gain supporters to help communicate the change to others. Be honest and sincere in all the messages; personal delivery of messages may be an excellent way to create support. Personal meetings to deliver the change message allows for questions and answers. Yes, personal meetings will take time, but it is an excellent approach to reaching the audience and developing the necessary support.

SUMMARY

Change is a process of moving from a current state of existence to a new state of existence. Lewin's (1951) change model expresses a behavioral evaluation of a situation that allows for the desire to change, the actual change, and the willingness to accept the new state. Lewin's model is the foundation of change theory. However, consider Kruger's (1996) iceberg model as a better way to describe and illustrate the complexity of change.

Kruger's (1996) model presents a visual depiction of the visible and hidden elements of change implementation.

Decker et al. (2012) concluded that the change initiative failure rate is likely between 50% to approximately 70%. Hughes (2011) did not find the empirical data to support the claim of 70% initiative failure. Any failure is possibly associated with a poor understanding of the "hidden" elements noted in Kruger's iceberg model, the lack of a systems perspective throughout the change initiative, and a partial or complete disregard of Kotter's 8-step model. Conversely, there is a higher chance of success if a change practitioner applies the concepts of change management, Kotter's change model, and robust project management techniques to any change initiative.

A robust understanding of a systems perspective is crucial to operating within a complex organization. Organizational systems are more than IT applications and network components. A complex organizational system consists of the formal and informal structure, the processes that constitute the work of the organization, and the culture of the organization. The organizational system always operates and may have a hidden influence on the outcome of a change initiative. An organizational system has interrelated and interdependent processes that work together to achieve organizational goals.

Kotter's (1996, 2012) 8-step model is an excellent approach to understanding and achieving change initiatives. The eight components of Kotter's model (Kotter, 1996, 2012) are:

- Justification
- Establishing Support
- Establishing a Connection between the Initiative and the Employees
- Effective Communication
- Managing Resistance to Change
- Practical Plans
- Momentum through Communication
- Institutionalization of the Initiative

REFERENCES

Busby, N. (2017). *The shape of change: A guide to planning, implementing and embedding organizational change.* New York, NY: Routledge.

Decker, P., Durand, R., Mayfield, C. O., McCormack, C., Skinner, D., & Perdue, G. (2012) Predicting implementation failure in organization change. *Journal of Organizational Culture, Communications and Conflict, 16*(2), 29–49.

Hughes, M. (2011). Do 70 per cent of all organizational change initiatives really fail? *Journal of Change Management*, 11(4), 451–464.

Kotter, J. P. (1996). Successful change and the force that drives it. *The Canadian Manager*, 21(3), 20–24.

Kotter, J. P. (2012). *Leading change*. Boston, MA: Harvard Business Review Press.

Kruger, W. (1996). Implementation: The core task of change management. *CEM Business Review*, 1, 77–96.

Lewin, K. (1951). *Field theory in social science*. New York: Harper & Row.

CHAPTER EXERCISES

1. **Kotter's Model**

   Why do you think Prof. Kotter focused on the eight steps identified in his model as necessary for successful change initiatives? Consider any examples from your experiences.

2. **BC Project: BIA**

   The business continuity department is planning to begin conducting a business impact analysis to determine what each business unit does, whom they interact with to perform functions, which relies on a particular business unit to conduct their work; in essence, the BIA should identify the business relationships (i.e., internal and external) and technical requirements for an organization. The project promises significant change implications for the organization. What are the change management issues associated with this project?

2

Strategic and Tactical Considerations of Change

LEARNING OBJECTIVES

The learning objectives of this chapter are:

- The Benefits of Change within an Organization
- Transformational Strategies
  - Focus on Quality Strategy
  - Search Conferences Strategy
  - Lead–Lag Strategy
  - Bottom-Up or Top-Down Strategy
  - Experimentation Strategy
- Interpersonal Skills
- Two Change Models for Consideration
  - Matrix of Change
  - Plan-Do-Check-Act Model

BENEFITS OF CHANGE

The benefits of change are considerable, with impacts occurring at both the organizational and individual levels. Any organization seeking to maintain a competitive edge must change to benefit from technological advances, market adjustments, and customer interests. When an improvement in the design or manufacturing process of a product prompts a change, there is a competitive need to change. If a new supplier offers a resource at a lower price, the logical result is a change in the supplier. If a resource component becomes unavailable, there might be an opportunity for a change into a new market or product.

Organizational changes allow people throughout the company to make new contacts and learn new skills. Change creates an opportunity for a new mindset within the organization; change requires a change in people. Leaders that support change initiatives foster dynamic flexibility in the workforce. The more practice people have with accepting and operating in a changing environment, the more capable they are of producing positive results. Change is not necessarily a bad thing – it depends on the point of view. For instance, when an organization looks to downsize or right size because of market fluctuations reducing the need to produce at the current level, there is often a great deal of stress. The workers know that people are likely to receive separation notices. Forward-thinking organizations seek to limit the loss of people. The loss of valuable skills, institutional knowledge, and loyalty can dramatically impact an organization. That is stressful and a negative change, but reducing the employee count might be the best thing for the organization. Outplacement services are often provided to help separated employees find new positions.

There are positive examples of change initiatives that can transform an organization. A simple change to how an organization processes financial statements can save substantial amounts of money and natural resources – look at paperless bank statements. Changing the dress code of an organization has a direct impact on the culture – many people love wearing business casual, and they are happier for the change. Consider the value of using electronic conferencing applications like Skype and WebEx to the organizational bottom line – vast amounts of travel money are saved each year. These change examples were transformational because of the broad impact on an organization.

CHANGE MANAGEMENT INTERVENTION

Coughlan and Rashford (2006) identified three critical processes for change to occur: first is the perception of the change, second is the assessment of the impact, and third is the response to the change. These three processes are mostly a linear progression from perception through response and involve psychological interactions between the workers and those proposing the change (Coughlan & Rashford, 2006). The perception of the change involves the individual, the lower-level group or team, and the organization as a whole. The perception of the change elements involves the meaning of the change as noted by the various levels and concerns, the degree of control by those affected by the change (organizational members), and finally, the degree of trust the organizational members have in those proposing the change (Coughlan & Rashford, 2006).

The assessment of the impact is predicated on the perception of the change. If the workers consider the change to endanger their job or any jobs, the change will likely be viewed negatively – this is just natural. For a positive assessment to be formed by those affected, the perception must be positive, those impacted by the change have a reasonable amount of control over the process, and there must be trust between the workers and those proposing the change (Coughlan & Rashford, 2006).

After the assessment of the impact of the change, there is the impact of the change. Again, this is not a simple single event, but a range of possibilities from wholehearted support to absolute resistance to the change (Coughlan & Rashford, 2006). The perception and assessment may be additive because people often cumulatively view iterative events, and the impact of a change is a complex issue. Coughlan and Rashford (2006) note that traditional change theory is centered on Lewin's (1948) approach to addressing change as a process of "unfreezing" the established organizational practice, "moving" to a new practice, and then "refreezing" to establish a new practice approach for the organization. However, there are perceived limitations to Lewin's approach in that change is often fast-paced, complex in implementation, and dynamic in the fluid nature of nonlinearity change initiatives requiring a modification that reflects additional considerations (Coughlan & Rashford, 2006).

There are four psychological stages to change as developed by Coughlan and Rashford (2006) that involve "denying" the change, "dodging" involvement in the change, "doing" the activities of the change, and "sustaining" the change; these build on Lewin's model (1948) and offer a more modern approach to realizing the complex nature of change. All of these stages are widespread sense-oriented and address natural reactions to change possibilities. The denying stage is where organizational members avoid accepting that the change will involve or affect them; the dodging stage involves the passive–aggressive avoidance of becoming involved when the change becomes evident that it will take place; the doing stage involves actual involvement in the change initiative; and finally, the sustaining stage is the reinforcement of the reasons for change and the importance for involvement (Coughlan & Rashford, 2006).

All of these stages are related to communications issues resulting from a poor understanding of the people involved, poor planning for the difficulties associated with resistance to change, or a failure to recognize the necessity of clear and complete information dissemination to the organization. Issuing a partial message is often worse than issuing no message; the partial message allows people to focus on that scrap of information and try to fill in the missing information, often resulting in a wrong conclusion or the worse possible outcome.

It is also valuable to appreciate and understand the nature of complex organizations. There are levels of an organization that facilitate interaction and influence. The lowest level is the interpersonal or small group interaction that has a tremendous personal impact within the organization. The department level in the middle area of the organization and has broad influence over a defined group. The highest level is the organization and may involve multiple locations across different countries. Each level has a dynamic interface with the other levels of the organization. Also, each level is affected by resistance to change for different reasons. However, regardless of the reason, the resistance must be addressed if the change initiative succeeds.

THE PROCESS FOR CHANGE

Change initiatives do not naturally spring into existence because there is extra funding. Coughlan & Rashford (2006) indicate these five stages or process activities of large-scale change within an organization: 1) determining the need; 2) establish the vision of the future; 3) assess the present state; 4) manage the change – beginning to end; 5) institutionalize the new state through sustaining the change. The stages are similar to Kotter's approach and are complimentary when developing a change initiative strategy. These stages use a cyclical approach to moving a change initiative from the earliest stages to the completed, sustaining stages. Each stage is critical to success; failure at any one stage will derail the project, perhaps permanently.

The first stage involves recognizing the need and benefit of a change. The need and benefit may involve political influence within the organization, as well as understanding the right time to suggest the project. For instance, if the organization is experiencing a poor economic return on investments and revenue indicators are performing poorly, it would be a bad idea to recommend using financial resources on a change that may not show a near-term return on investment. Timing is everything in an organization.

The second stage involves establishing the vision of the future state in the people's minds in the organization. The second stage is essentially the process of developing a shared vision, as discussed by Senge (2006). Establishing a shared vision is a tremendously powerful method of gaining active participation within an organization. People begin to "see" the future through the constant reminders of what will be after the change is completed. Remember, not all members of the organization will share the same perspective within the organization. A line worker will likely have a different perspective than the CEO of the organization.

The third stage is to fully assess the present state of affairs in the organization, to include all levels of the organization. Assessing the present state allows the change agents to understand the situation above, below, and laterally of the specific business unit involved in the proposed change. It is necessary to look up and down the organizational structure to ensure an accurate picture is established and a crystal clear understanding of the people is determined. Resistance to change is one of the most critical issues surrounding a change initiative; it must be addressed before the change begins.

The fourth stage is to manage the change initiative from beginning to end. As noted in the third stage, it is necessary to prepare for resistance by preventing it from starting. It is necessary to include organizational members, perhaps all of them, in the change initiative to ensure inclusion in the discussions and the planning activities. Resistance to change is addressed in the next section of this paper.

The fifth and final stage is the new state's institutionalization by sustaining the change within the organization. Institutionalization involves the marketing efforts developed in the early stages to communicate the need for the project; there is a need to communicate the change's ongoing value. Showing people how they and the organization benefit from the change are essential to fix the change in the people's minds – remind them why it was necessary. This stage involves organizational learning and relates to Lewin's (1948) refreezing stage and the sustaining stage identified by Coughlan and Rashford (2006). It is valuable to note that change is a learning process in all organizations and is continuously taking place in many forms. Coughlan and Rashford (2006) indicate the importance of feedback activities throughout the process of change, focusing

27

on the behaviors and actions, the strategic underpinnings of the behaviors, and finally, the strategies' intentions, as mentioned earlier. Constant review and honest assessments of the actions will significantly benefit the organization.

TRANSFORMATIONAL STRATEGIES

Transformational change involves organization-wide initiatives affecting most employees and involves new ways of doing things to include new behaviors (Carlström, 2012). It is essential to understand the transformative change initiative strategic approach used to realize the change. The change initiative determines the appropriateness of a strategic approach. The focus on the strategic approach to achieve transformative change acknowledges the challenges associated with all change initiatives. For example, strategic organizational values lead to transformational change through participative efforts (Munro, 1992). The strategic approach drives the achievement of a transformative change by identifying, planning, communicating, implementing, and monitoring a change initiative.

FOCUS ON QUALITY STRATEGY

The focus on quality has been a long-standing concern for artisans and anyone producing and using a product, including intangible products such as electronic information (i.e., video, audio, and written/graphic presentations). The customer, through the comparison of a perceived actual product against the perceived intended product (expectations), against the perception of the competitor's product, determines the quality (Beach, 2006). Ensure that the change initiative is presented and perceived as a quality market that changes as a quality endeavor.

The illusion of the quality dynamic appears to be the organization's desire to create the best product or service. However, the real driving force is the customer's perception of the product. The client's demand for a perceived product is the measure against which the organization strives to achieve quality; the client's perception of expectations is the measure of quality. If the customer thinks something is a quality product, the perception translates into a quality product. Any marketing campaign uses the dynamic of perception (i.e., the idea of quality) as the catalyst to convince the customer that an image or idea is quality.

Beach (2006) describes the Quality Improvement Strategy (QIS) as the measure of the perceptions through a questionnaire to capture the above relationship's data in the quantifiable form to allow for statistical analysis of the quality dynamic. The satisfaction of the customer is the core issue under discussion. If the customer is satisfied with a product or service, then the organization has achieved quality. Naturally, the competition between organizations to provide demonstrable improvements and added features to products to win customer satisfaction is constant.

The quality strategy is the acknowledged relationship between the customer's perception of a product or service, against the actual product or service, against the competition's perceived product. The perception is the measuring stick, and the point at which the dissatisfaction of the product and the competitor's product come together is the basis for change (Beach, 2006). Transformative change occurs to address the lack of quality. However, in reality, it is the quest to achieve a balance between perceptions and products. A Seinfeld episode discussed this relationship when Kramer started working at an advertising agency developing an ad campaign, and he stated they sell the sizzle, not the steak. The perception of the steak was at issue, not the actual steak product. The transformative change for an organization seeks to make the necessary modifications to improve the product's perceived quality.

There are also practical manufacturing issues that involve change, such as producing the perceived quality product for the lowest cost. Achieving the balance between cost-effective resources, assembly, and marketing is just as important as the product's image. A Cadillac is a well-made vehicle, and the perception tends to equate to one of quality. However, General Motors must produce the vehicle economically if it is to achieve viability as a marketable product. The balance between product perception and cost-effective creation is the basis for typical transformative initiatives at organizations; the product or service can be anything that is of value to a customer. Even though the discussion has focused on physical items, the risk-based services provided by internal company departments are the same. Perception is often referred to as reality; people believe the perception as reality.

SEARCH CONFERENCES STRATEGY

The search conference strategy to transformational change is based on a whole systems approach to addressing a systemic, strategic change initiative through large-scale employee involvement in identifying and

29

planning the modification (Stone, 1996). The advantage of using this approach to plan a change within an organization is the involvement of a vast number of people who know the organization; the employees involved are more than just senior leaders. The change initiatives coming out of a search conference may include any modification; identifying the need and scope of the change is fundamental to understanding what is required to improve the organization. Stone (1996) indicated the use of the future search conference to identify and plan transformational change at a federal agency (i.e., U. S. Department of Agriculture) that involved holistic change efforts, including the vision of the change and how to approach the initiative.

Perhaps one of the most critical aspects of this strategy is the understanding that transformative change throughout the organization requires a fundamental shift in the values, focus, and culture of the organization (Stone, 1996). The approach indicated by Stone (1996) for the federal agency involved five necessary components in achieving the level of transformative change desired for systemic influences. The five elements are a clear vision of the outcome, the consensus, and commitment of a majority number of organizational stakeholders (i.e., internal and external) actively seeking to achieve the change and outcome, and the acknowledgment and empowerment of the entire workforce to achieve the change (Stone, 1996). Also, the alignment and compatibility of the systems and processes with the change vision are crucial. The initiative's implementation process must continuously be measured against the organization's real-time status (Stone, 1996).

The search conference strategy involves all participants' open and honest involvement to achieve a holistic approach to viewing organizational needs. The participants must possess a good knowledge of the organization's systems and processes, including internal and external stakeholder demands upon the organization. Developing a strategic, transformative change initiative is achieved when the entire organization is involved, supportive, and moving forward with a unified vision of the expected outcome.

LEAD–LAG STRATEGY

The lead–lag strategy to transformative change is an acknowledgment of the time necessary to acquire and provide resources to a project. Lead time is a common phrase when attempting to collect the supplies for a project; participants often hear that the supplies will take weeks to arrive at the facility. For instance, Dow Chemical uses advanced forecasting to identify and project the availability and demand of resources for products, as well as the demand for products (Sweeney, 2010). The real value of Dow's analytical approach was not on producing volumes of numeric data, but rather the focus on the lead–lag (i.e., input–output) relationship to economic demands and the need for input resources and external output demands (Sweeney, 2010).

The lead-lag strategic approach in transformative change focuses on the various resources associated with initiatives and the external commitments an organization may have to stakeholders. The timely acquisition of resources and the preparation of distribution of the products will result in considerable cost savings because items arrive and ship when best suited to the situation. For instance, knowing when to ship a new high-profile product for an expected customer demand (e.g., the advertisement of a new soft drink before a holiday weekend) is highly desirable. It allows the product to arrive in time to take the best advantage of the economic market. Reynolds and Yetton (2015) describe the balance of internal indicators (i.e., lead) and external indicators (i.e., lag) to address the lead-lag cyclical supply and demand relationship.

The strategy's primary criteria require a clear understanding of the organizational resources and the ability to achieve infrastructure capabilities. The knowledge associated with the resources is generated from collecting data about the change initiative's organizational systems and processes. Analyzing the data allows for a robust understanding to identify the lead and lag times involved in resource-product management. Long-term or longitudinal trend data are an excellent method to obtain the necessary information to view historical lead and lag instances. However, forecasting models are needed to get future knowledge.

BOTTOM-UP OR TOP-DOWN STRATEGY

The bottom-up and top-down strategy is a combination of two management styles; bottom-up is decentralized management, and top-down is the centralized management approach. According to Tsai and Beverton (2007), the top-down approach of decision-making allows the senior management to use the inherent power of the position to focus the organization's resources on developing shared involvement (i.e., commitment to perform) to a project. The top-down approach provides for the explanation of the strategic rationale of a change initiative. An advantage of the top-down or centralized strategic approach is the central management's ability to view the entire organization when making major wide-scale decisions (Tsai & Beverton, 2007).

The significance of this central decision-making ability is evident when viewed in comparison with the bottom-up or decentralized strategic approach. A decentralized decision-making focus is centered on the specific business unit and not the entire organization, and that limitation is a weakness. The limited focus inherent in decentralized decisions creates a lack of holistic vision and decisions that may benefit the lower-level business unit may be inadequate for the larger organization. An example of this is strategic sourcing agreements that provide low-cost travel for the organization while sacrificing the better periodic deal for a single person through a cut-rate online site. The decentralized strategic approach has advantages that allow for the justified use of the strategy.

There is considerable flexibility and encouraged involvement in decentralized management, which profoundly influences the efficient use of resources and business unit performance (Tsai & Beverton, 2007). The focus of business unit management on the unit's issues allows for a more informed local concentration. Therefore, the decisions are more likely to result in an increased benefit to the business unit. Tsai and Beverton (2007) indicate a significant relationship that is at the heart of the decentralized model; decentralization is democratic and allows for increased involvement of the employees closest to the decision-makers.

Transformative change initiatives using the top-down and bottom-up strategy has the advantage of benefiting from two different decision-making approaches that can work together when implemented. The centralized approach takes a wide-scale view of issues. It can consolidate information from the lower business units in an organization. The decentralized approach can focus the necessary energies on the business unit and create the required benefit. Together, both approaches work nicely to provide the organization's different views and focus the required resources at the appropriate level on providing the best results.

EXPERIMENTATION STRATEGY

The experimental strategy to achieving transformational change at an organization relies on the concept that the change produces a competitive edge that the organization uses to gain market share of some advantage over the competition (Krokaew, & Ussahawanitchakit, 2015). The pharmaceutical companies devote extensive research and development resources to achieve a transformational change in the respective industry and organization if successful. A new drug has the potential for considerable profits for the organization. However, there are also risks associated with new medicines. Assessing the side effects of a drug and the possible percentage of occurrences in the population requires a leadership decision to market the new product or to conduct further studies. The balance between bringing a new product to market and not taking the chance on serious liability issues developing from the item are significant strategic matters.

The value of the experimentation approach to strategic change is the highest level of risk management. Determining the amounts of resources to devote to research against the potential payout at the end of the effort is career-changing for many executives. The combination of transformative leadership, product innovativeness, and market performance are significantly related (Krokaew & Ussahawanitchakit, 2015). The use of the experimental strategy to transform an organization is possible and potentially significant in economic outcomes.

INTERPERSONAL SKILLS

Interpersonal skills are critical to establishing a meaningful relationship with people, thereby achieving the desired change initiative. Many professionals focus on developing their knowledge base associated with their specialty (e.g., business continuity professional). While establishing and maintaining professional expertise is essential, the often overlooked "soft-skills" is just as valuable to make the necessary connection with people. Change management is dependent upon the human connection between people, and interpersonal skills are necessary to make that connection. Make eye contact with the person or people in the audience. Speak clearly and directly – avoid jargon and big words. Do not speak down to the audience, but do not try to sound smart – be yourself. Be honest and sincere when discussing issues. Tailor the message to the audience and identify the issues needed to gain the audience's trust and interest. Make the audience a partner in the change initiative process – be friendly.

TWO CHANGE MODELS FOR CONSIDERATION

There are numerous change models for change management profession-als to consider when viewing a change initiative. While there are many models available, most require an advanced level of knowledge and expe-rience to gain any benefit from those models. In Appendix D, there is a list of selected references for further reading. The Hollman et al. (2007) change handbook is an excellent resource for those looking for additional advanced information.

The selection of the model is dependent upon many issues such as the specifics of the project, the resources associated with the project (e.g., time, location, the scope of the change), the professional's familiarity with the model, and the appropriateness of the model. Change professionals may favor a particular model because of comfort and familiarity, but that does not mean the model is appropriate for all change initiatives and organiza-tional environments.

If the model is flexible and accommodating modification and the change professional prefers that model because of previous outcomes, it may be an acceptable model to use. There are many change models because there are many approaches to implementing change based on the wide variety of organizations and situations. Otherwise, change profes-sionals would use a single model.

Two models have been selected as examples to illustrate the diverse scope of models for use in change initiatives. The first model is the Matrix of Change, and the second model is the Organizational Resilience Man-agement (ORM) System Flow Diagram – Plan-Do-Check-Act model. Both models are potent examples of the variety of choices, and each has certain advantages and disadvantages for use in practical change projects. It is unfair to say one is better than the other; it is more appropriate to say that each is valuable in the right situation.

A change model helps focus organizational resources and under-standing to address a particular initiative. The collaboration of Human Resources and Organizational Development teams is an example of a focused division of labor, dynamic creativeness by employees benefiting from shared visions and resources (Moultry-Belcher, 2010). A change ini-tiative may require specialized personnel, and the change may, in part, be associated with employee selection (Akhtar & Cozic, 2010). However, before the actual change models may be discussed, it is necessary to dis-cuss the fundamental aspects of change management. Each model is a limited approach to accomplishing a change. However, the framework surrounding the concept of change is the critical construct that allows a model to function appropriately.

MATRIX OF CHANGE

The first change model is the Matrix of Change. The matrix is more of a practical tool for managers to use when planning and assessing change processes. It has the appearance of a mathematical matrix closely aligned to a decision-oriented approach to considering a change. Even a cursory review of the matrix will indicate that a user must have a thorough understanding of the organization for this model to be of value. The subjective assessment of processes requires an in-depth understanding of success.

The matrix is a powerful tool to accomplish a change initiative. However, it is not a simple approach to pick up and use with confidence. The Matrix of Change is highly detailed-oriented and relatively complex because of the necessary detail. As shown in Figures 2.1 and 2.2, there is a great deal of cross-referencing and complex identification of processes and problems. The forecasting of practice value and cross-referenced relationships requires careful thought and a thorough understanding of the organization. That is not unusual for a complex change initiative. However, it is something that professionals must appreciate when considering this model for an initiative.

An exciting aspect of this model is the identification of the interaction of processes, as indicated in Figure 2.1. The positive and negative symbols relate to the level of complimentary, weak, or no interaction between the processes (Brynjoifsson, Renshaw, & Van Alstyne, 1997). The relationship indicates an insightful aspect of the model in that the processes of the system are some of the most potent components of the system. Failing to consider these relationships will likely have negative implications for any change initiative.

As shown in Figures 2.1 and 2.2, the Matrix of Change model reflects the complex nature of organizations with an acknowledgment of existing primary and sub-processes, relative to the target practices with a numeric assessment of the interaction (Brynjoifsson, Renshaw, & Van Alstyne, 1997). For this model to be of value, it is necessary to thoroughly understand the business unit (a sub-unit or the whole organization) so that meaningful information can be used in the model matrix. The more detailed and accurate the matrix's information, the more accurate the outcome of the model's change process. Note the positive and negative numbers in Figure 2.1;

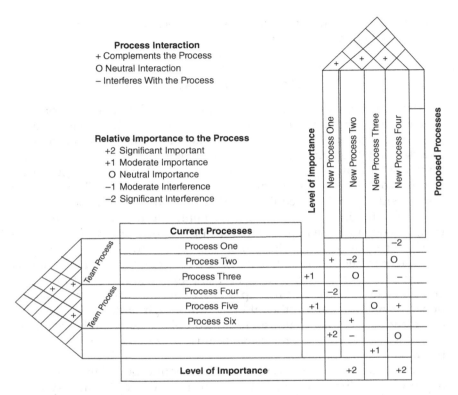

Figure 2.1 Matrix of Change Model – Completed Form (Adapted from Brynjoifsson et al. (1997)).

they are subjective assessments of the importance of the practices identified in the matrix. These assessments require an excellent understanding of the organization and the processes being assessed. It is appropriate to note that failure to understand the implications of the subjective determination of the importance of the processes may likely have undesirable consequences for the model's usefulness.

Understanding the organization to use a particular model is not unique; it is necessary to thoroughly understand the organization when assessing a change initiative. When conducting any assessment, it is a standard requirement that the organization must be thoroughly understood to make the correct recommendations and adjustments to a change initiative.

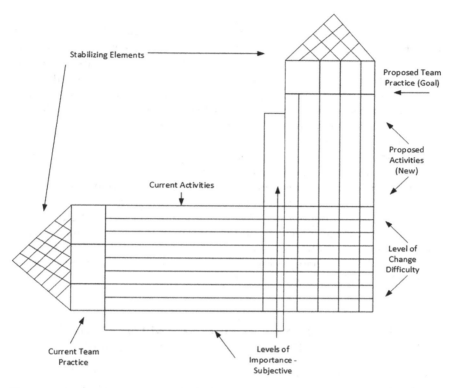

Figure 2.2 Matrix of Change Model – Blank Form (Adapted from Brynjoifsson et al. (1997)).

CHANGE INTERVENTION USABILITY

The Matrix of Change model appears to be best considered for smaller-sized projects due to the level of detail necessary for the completion of the matrix. Attempting to document an entire organization with this matrix seems more complicated than warranted and likely to fail because of an inability to manage the complex relationships. Using the matrix repeatedly throughout the organization may be possible. However, again the difficulty in managing the complex nature of process relationships will increase the likelihood of failure. Consider Figure 2.2 and the necessary identification of an organization's processes and identifying the interacting processes; the accurate documentation of the relationships is often unmanageable for a large-scale organizational change.

This model is much more applicable for a small-scale change initiative because of the opportunity to detail the minute relationships that impact the interrelatedness of the processes and the sub-processes. This model can take advantage of the highly detail-oriented nature of sophisticated system design. The collection of detailed information on the processes must be obtained by a person familiar with the business unit being assessed. The association of current practice and future (change initiative) practice will again require people familiar with the change processes. Taking an inclusive approach to the change initiative is commonplace and logical, especially when it is valuable to obtain a comprehensive view of the processes to ensure nothing is missed.

The decision to use this model is grounded in the model's fundamental aspects and the information necessary to bring value to the model. Small projects will benefit best from the model because of the ability to detail the processes' interrelatedness. This model will be challenging to use on large projects that involve large business units with highly complex processes. The change practitioner will be expected to determine the appropriate model for a change initiative.

ORGANIZATIONAL RESILIENCE MANAGEMENT SYSTEM – PLAN-DO-CHECK-ACT MODEL

The ORM system flow diagram change model used in the ORM (ASIS International, 2017) is very similar to the Whole-Scale Change model presented by James and Tolchinsky (2007). The critical component of both approaches is an ongoing process of continual improvement through organizational learning. Figure 2.3 indicates the cyclical, iterative progressive movement design from component to component as directed by the arrows. The activities in each box are identified and addressed through the Plan-Do-Check-Act cycle indicated in Figure 2.4.

The significant difference between the Whole-Scale Change approach and the ORM system flow diagram change model is the model's scope. Both are fully capable of addressing change on the organizational level. However, the ORM approach is designed to work at any level within the organization. Instead of focusing only on the entire organization, the ORM design works very well at smaller organization levels. However, organizational resilience is not limited to only the impacted organizational group or level; it is more holistic and interrelated through the entire organization.

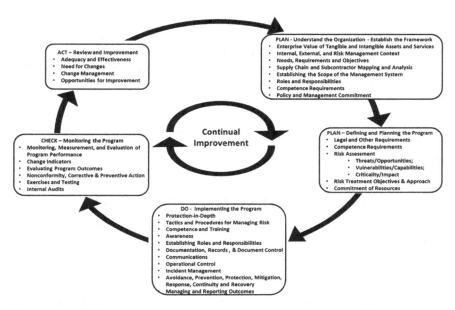

Figure 2.3 ORM System Flow Diagram Model (ASIS International, 2017, p. xix).

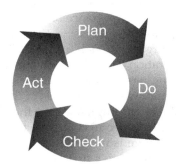

Figure 2.4 Plan-Do-Check-Act Model (Adapted from ASIS International, 2017, p. 107).

For instance, if a single business department is used for the change initiative, the change effects are limited to that department. However, there are serious flaws with this sort of limitation because of the inherent influence of processes and the interrelatedness of complex organizations; the selected department surely has external stakeholders and vendors that should be involved in the ORM change and will not benefit from the change because of their being excluded from the change. The ORM model can be used on a single sub-unit of the organization for a limited effect change. However, it can affect change in the entire organization.

For this model to be useful, it is imperative for senior management to fully support the change initiative and become involved in the process. Senior management involvement is necessary even if the change is intended for only a team or department because of the nature of organizational performance assessments; if senior management is not supportive, the workers will not see the change's value and will not spend the time on an unsanctioned project.

CHANGE INTERVENTION USABILITY

The ORM model is designed for a particular change initiative, the implementation of organizational resilience management in an organization seeking to improve the organization's adaptive capacity in a complex and changing environment (ASIS International, 2017). As noted earlier, the ORM model is similar to the Whole-Scale model and can be used as such for other change initiatives. For an organizational resilience implementation initiative, certain expectations allow the model to function effectively. For instance, senior management must fully and actively support the change initiative to communicate the importance of the change to the employees.

One of the most powerful aspects of the ORM model is continual improvement through organizational learning. The development of a shared vision and organizational learning allows an organization to become truly great and instill long-term change initiatives (Senge, 2006). Through the involvement of the employees at all levels of the organizations and the acceptance of responsibility for implementing the change initiative, there is the opportunity for a fundamental change in the organization's culture. Organizational culture change is not a natural or common outcome. The model allows for the organization's full involvement or the involvement of the smaller team/department when a scaled-down approach is desired.

The major components of the model move through a cycle of progression starting with knowing the organization; followed by identifying and establishing the policy surrounding the initiative; followed next by planning the details of the change; then the actual implementation of the change; followed by checking for conformance and corrective action in addressing any feedback issues; finally, there is a comprehensive management review of the change, along with the ongoing continual improvement throughout the entire process (ASIS International, 2017).

Throughout the entire process, there is the Plan-Do-Check-Act cycle (i.e., Figure 2.4) taking place at each stage, with the inherent understanding that the model is cyclical, iterative, and process-oriented. If there is a problem at any stage of the model, it is perfectly fine to go back and make adjustments; this is not a linear process. It may be helpful to picture the diagram from Figure 2.4 decreased in size and placed next to each rectangle in Figure 2.3; this model is exceptionally fluid and flexible.

The real value of the Plan-Do-Check-Act cycle is the continual process of learning throughout the change process. Continual improvement is a clearly stated component of the model. However, continual organizational learning is an inherent expectation of the process. As noted earlier in this paper, learning from events and new norms is a critical part of the change process. Notice in Figure 2.3, the process does not end but continues to proceed through the change model in an unending cycle. The Plan-Do-Check-Act cycle allows organizations to maintain and sustain the currency of the change initiative. Change never really ends. Figure 2.5 provides a useful explanation for the Plan-Do-Check-Act model illustrated in Figure 2.4.

PLAN (establish the management system)	Establish management system policy, objectives, processes, and procedures relevant to managing operations and improving risk management to deliver results in accordance with an organization's overall policies and objectives.
DO (implement and operate the management system)	Implement and operate the management system policy, controls, processes, and procedures.
CHECK (monitor and review the management system)	Assess and measure process performance against management system policy, objectives, and practical experience and report the results to management for review.
ACT (maintain and improve the management system)	Take corrective and preventive actions, based on the results of the internal management system audit and management review, to achieve continual improvement of the management system.

Figure 2.5 Plan-Do-Check-Act Model – Descriptive Notes (ASIS International, 2017, p. 107).

ADVANTAGES AND DISADVANTAGES
OF THE CHANGE MODELS

As noted throughout this paper, each model has certain advantages and disadvantages. The matrix of change is more of a practical tool for managers to use when planning and assessing processes for change. It has the advantage of having a mathematical matrix's appearance aligned to a process matrix used to consider the change. The matrix uses a sophisticated approach requiring a user that has a thorough understanding of the organization for this model to be of value. The subjective assessment of processes requires an in-depth understanding of the success criteria. The subjective assessment is both an advantage and a disadvantage.

While the matrix is a powerful tool to accomplish a change initiative, it is not a simple approach to pick up and use with confidence. The matrix of change is detail-oriented and requires an excellent understanding of the organization and the related processes associated with the change process. Again, this requirement is certainly a disadvantage, but may also be an advantage as it forces those involved in managing the change to be fully involved.

The model is much more applicable for a small-scale change initiative because of the opportunity to detail the minute relationships that impact the interrelatedness of the processes and the sub-processes. Large-scale projects will likely become too complicated for reasonable use. It is undoubtedly an advantage for the model to use the highly detail-oriented nature of sophisticated system design; it is also subject to failure because of the complexity of the design. The collection of detailed information on the processes requires a person familiar with the business unit being assessed, and this again is both an advantage and disadvantage because it relies on limited personnel resources in a business unit.

The ORM system flow diagram (i.e., change model) is very similar to the Whole-Scale Change model. There is a real advantage because the Whole-Scale Change model is well established and is currently used (James & Tolchinsky, 2007). The critical advantage of both approaches is an ongoing process of continual improvement through organizational learning. This ongoing feedback loop allows for constant monitoring and adjustment throughout the process of change.

While the Whole-Scale Change approach is focused on large-scale, organization-wide change, the ORM system flow diagram has the flexibility to scale down to smaller business units if necessary. However, the

ORM model was intended for system-wide change to take advantage of the interrelatedness of internal and external supply chains and vendors' complex processes. This model takes advantage of using a systems approach to managing change in a complex environment.

The development of a shared vision and organizational learning allows an organization to benefit from the change initiative (Senge, 2006). This continual improvement through organizational learning is a fundamental underpinning of the model and perhaps the most critical aspect of the entire process. The Plan-Do-Check-Act cycle is another aspect of the continual process of learning throughout the change process.

SUMMARY

Any organization seeking to maintain a competitive edge must change to benefit from technological advances, market adjustments, and customer interests. Organizational changes allow people throughout the company to make new interpersonal relationships and learn new skills. Change creates an opportunity for a new mindset within the organization; change requires a change in people. Leaders that support change initiatives foster dynamic flexibility in the workforce. The more practice people have with accepting and operating in a changing environment, the more capable they are of producing positive results.

Transformational change involves organization-wide initiatives affecting most of the employees and involves new ways of doing things to include new behaviors (Carlström, 2012). It is important to understand the transformative change initiative strategic approach used to realize the change. The change initiative determines the appropriateness of a strategic approach. The focus on the strategic approach to achieve transformative change acknowledges the challenges associated with all change initiatives. The strategic approach drives the achievement of a transformative change by identifying, planning, communicating, implementing, and monitoring a change initiative.

Interpersonal skills are critical to establishing a meaningful relationship with people, thereby achieving the desired change initiative. Many professionals focus on developing their knowledge base associated with their specialty. While establishing and maintaining professional expertise is essential, the often overlooked "soft-skills" is just as critical to making the necessary connection with people. Change management is dependent upon the human connection between people, and interpersonal skills are necessary to make that connection. Make the audience a partner in the change initiative process – be friendly.

The change matrix and the Plan-Do-Check-Act cycle models are powerful and useful change tools to facilitate the change initiative's completion. Both models have advantages and disadvantages, and it is necessary to understand the models to ensure appropriate selection in complex change environments. The models are highly useful in complex environments but may not be appropriate in all situations.

The Matrix of Change is appropriate for smaller, more contained change projects that allow the matrix to benefit from the detailed information needed to complete the matrix. The interrelatedness of complex processes conventional in dynamic systems will be challenging to manage.

The ORM System Flow Diagram – Plan-Do-Check-Act model is well suited for large-scale organizations to small-scale business units. This model was designed for implementing organizational resilience. However, it can be modified quite quickly because it is based on the Whole-Scale Change model presented by James and Tolchinsky (2007).

Senge (2006) discusses the value of developing a shared vision and organizational learning experience as a benefit from the change initiative. The ORM model uses continual improvement and organizational learning as a fundamental underpinning of the model; this is probably the most critical aspect of the entire process.

Each model is exceptionally well suited for the purpose it was designed for and has a certain level of flexibility to include more change options. The Matrix of change model is less suited but still very powerful in the right situation. Each has specific requirements for practical use and, therefore, limitations. However, the issues are treatable if the OD professionals fully understand the model and the organization.

The strategies discussed herein are effective methods for achieving transformative change. Each strategy works fine as the primary approach to change. However, there are opportunities for combining strategies synergistically to achieve transformative change. An example of two strategic approaches working together is a quality improvement as a strategy and catalyst for developing team efforts to modify systems and processes and supported through a top-down strategic approach to transformative change (LeBrasseur, Whissell, & Ojha, 2002).

The strategy depends on the interpersonal skills and the change manager's ability to use the change models. Change managers that are advanced in their use of the models will likely have better results;

there is nothing wrong with taking a straightforward approach. The change agent must make a positive and personal connection with the audience to gain trust and participation throughout the change process. Interpersonal skills will make the difference between the audience wanting to become involved and an audience that is doubtful about the change initiative.

REFERENCES

Akhtar, M. F., & Cozic, C. (2010). Unleashing innovation through HR/OD collaboration. *OD. Practitioner*, 42(4), 47–51.

ASIS International. (2017). *Security and resilience in organizations and their supply chains – Requirements with guidance (ASIS ORM.1-2017)*. Alexandria, VA: American National Standards Institute.

Beach, L. R. (2006). *Leadership and the art of change: A practical guide to organizational change*. Thousand Oaks, CA: Sage.

Brynjoifsson, E., Renshaw, A., & Van Alstyne, M. (1997). The matrix of change. *Sloan Management Review*, 38(2), 37–54. Retrieved from http://sloanreview.mit.edu/article/the-matrix-of-change/

Carlström, E. D. (2012). Strategies for change: Adaptation to new accounting conditions. *Journal of Accounting & Organizational Change*, 8(1), 41–61.

Coughlan, D., & Rashford, N. (2006). *Organizational change and strategy: An interlevel dynamics approach*. New York, NY: Routledge.

Hollman, P., Devane, T., & Cady, S. (Eds.). (2007). *The change handbook: The definitive resource on today's best methods for engaging whole systems* (2nd ed.). San Francisco, CA: Berrett Koehler.

James, S., & Tolchinsky, P. (2007). World-Scale Change. In P. Hollman, T. Devane, and S. Cady (Eds.), *The change handbook: The definitive resource on today's best methods for engaging whole systems*, (2nd ed., pp. 162–178). San Francisco, CA: Berrett Koehler.

Krokaew, Y., & Ussahawanitchakit, P. (2015). New product development creativity and marketing sustainability: Evidence from instant and convenience foods in Thailand. *The Business and Management Review*, 7(1), 242–255.

LeBrasseur, R., Whissell, R., & Ojha, A. (2002). Organisational learning, transformational leadership and implementation of continuous quality improvement in Canadian hospitals. *Australian Journal of Management*, 27(2), 141–162.

Lewin, K. (1948). Group decision and social change. Reprinted in M. Gold (ed.) *The complete social scientist: A Kurt Lewin Reader*, (pp. 265–284). Washington, DC: American Psychological Association.

Moultry-Belcher, L. (2010). Advantages & disadvantages of collaboration in the workplace. *Demand Media*. Retrieved from http://smallbusiness.chron.com/advantages-disadvantages-collaboration-workplace-20965.html

Munro, R. (1992). Enabling participative change: The impact of a strategic value. *International Studies of Management & Organization*, 21(4), 52–65.

Reynolds, P., & Yetton, P. (2015). Aligning business and IT strategies in multi-business organizations. *Journal of Information Technology*, 30(2), 101–118.

Senge, P. (2006). *The fifth discipline: The art and practice of the learning organization.* New York, NY: Doubleday.

Stone, D. (1996). Leading edge methodology using future search conferences to achieve the Aphis vision. *National Productivity Review (1986–1998)*, 16(1), 57–63.

Sweeney, J. (2010). Back to the future. *Business Finance*, 16(3), 10.

Tsai, Y., & Beverton, S. (2007). Top-down management: An effective tool in higher education? *The International Journal of Educational Management*, 21(1), 6–16.

CHAPTER EXERCISES

1. **Physical Security: PACS**

   The director of security of a mid-sized financial organization has decided to begin the process of implementing electronic, physical access control for the organization. The CEO has approved the project and has provided verbal support during the executive committee meeting approving the project. What are the change management issues associated with this project?

2. **Business Impact Analysis: General Risk**

   You have been assigned to meet with the managers of the HR team to discuss conducting business impact analyses (BIA) for the team. The managers are very busy, and they are reluctant to agree to participate in the BIAs. The information gained from the BIAs is used by several departments, such as business continuity, security, ITDR, and risk management. How would you go about gaining their participation in the BIAs?

3

Resistance to Change

LEARNING OBJECTIVES

The learning objectives of this chapter are:

- Resistance to Change
- Reasons for Resistance to Change
- Methods to Overcome Resistance to Change
- Change Failures

RESISTANCE TO CHANGE

Change is an essential activity within an organization seeking to maintain a competitive edge over other organizations, as well as maintaining the necessary flexibility during emergencies. While change may be necessary for a successful organization to adapt, survive, and flourish, it is usually difficult and stressful to achieve. Resistance to change is common because it requires people to accept the change from both a personal and professional perspective. It is not unusual for a person to fear being judged harshly or unfairly during a change period within an organization. This fear may result from new business strategies, new approaches to address existing or potential concerns, proposed improvements or thought processes, and performance expectations, creating a level of stress that may have implications at work and home.

Resistance to change is a complex and multifaceted challenge to institutional change initiatives. Resistance may occur at any level of the organization and result from different reasons relative to the individual, organizational employee(s) (e.g., Blank, 1990; Agócs, 1997; Lane, McCormack, & Richardson, 2013). Organization-wide resistance may occur from the institutional level (Agócs, 1997), or there may be resistance because of an implementation-related issue associated with the manager (Gilley, Gilley, & McMillan, 2009). Poor communication or a lack of information may create severe problems and result in resistance to change through organizational uncertainty (Kennedy, 2011). There is also a possibility that senior management leaders will be resistant to the change because of the unknown risk associated with the change (Lane et al., 2013). However, failures associated with a change initiative are typically the result of human actions, or the lack thereof, and not by technical issues (Palmer, 2004).

Understanding the methods for overcoming resistance to change is valuable to promote the change initiative's more effective implementation. Addressing the specifics of overcoming resistance to change should be of great interest to practitioners seeking direct methods to accomplish the desired goal. The practical application of these methods should assist in real-world implementation toward affecting resistance to change. In particular, the disciplines of business, security, emergency, and disaster management will benefit from the knowledge presented herein. These disciplines seek improvements in implementing various initiatives to achieve risk management, emergency preparedness, or organizational effectiveness. An improved understanding of the methods for overcoming resistance to change should greatly help address change resistance within an organization.

Modern organizations routinely encounter dynamic environmental changes requiring a change from the organization to ensure survivability (Avey, Wernsing, & Luthans, 2008; Holt, Dorey, Bailey, & Low, 2009). With change also comes the potential for resistance.

REASONS FOR RESISTANCE TO CHANGE

As noted by Coughlan and Rashford (2006), the trust of management and those leading the change initiative is of critical concern. Cynicism may result from mistrust of leadership, change agents, and even themselves creating a form of resistance to the change (Kennedy, 2011); this is more of organizational cancer than just a single project issue and may have implications for the larger organization. There is a difference between skepticism in the change initiative (resistance to the actual change), and a cynical view of leadership/management, resulting in resistance to the change (Stanley, Meyer, & Topolnytsky, 2005). Distrust of management is an inherent problem within the organization and may be reflected in perceptions of projects. Apart from the change initiative, the trust issue must be resolved for the organization to be effective.

It is also necessary to understand that resistance to change may occur at different levels of the organization, and therefore should be addressed at different levels. An organization-wide concern requires a significant effort that has repercussions throughout the organization. For instance, the CEO may have to gather the entire organization and explain or discuss the problem to impart a powerful message fully. The department leader may address a department-level resistance concern and an individual-level issue addressed by a supervisor.

The exchange of information between organizational members may support or destroy a change initiative; the power of communication cannot be understated. Failure on the part of the leader to effectively communicate and motivate organizational members is a common reason for change initiatives to fail through resistance on the part of disillusioned employees (Gilley et al., 2009). A self-perpetuating cycle of resistance may follow because of reinforcement in beliefs of failure (Holt et al., 2009). Again, communication is the crux of the issue and must be resolved before a change initiative can be successful.

Organizational change and any associated resistance are not necessarily constant or uniform in rationale. Resistance may come from various levels of the organization and may be the result of various concerns of organizational members (e.g., Blank, 1990; Agócs, 1997; Lane, McCormack, & Richardson, 2013). Resistance to change may come from institutional resistance to change (Agócs, 1997), poor implementation of the change initiative by the project/program manager (Gilley, Gilley, & McMillan, 2009), from a sense of general organizational uncertainty about the change (Kennedy, 2011), or resistance by senior leadership to avoid the unknown risk of potential opportunity (Lane et al., 2013).

Palmer (2004) confirmed that change failures are caused by human actions or lack of action, and not by technical issues. Therefore, resistance to change may occur throughout an organization with the members of the

49

organization at the heart of the issue. General uncertainty about a change initiative may result from cynicism, dubious trust of leadership, and the employee's lack of confidence in each other (Kennedy, 2011). Uncertainty is a more pervasive issue within the organization and is a serious problem beyond the current change initiative.

Stanley, Meyer, and Topolnytsky (2005) identify the difference between skeptical resistance to proposed change (doubt in the project) and cynical resistance to the change (doubt or mistrust in management). Effective organizational communication is a crucial component of resistance. However, there is a subjective nature to a cynicism that may begin to influence leadership through continual change implementation failure and should be addressed to prevent worsening issues (Stanley et al., 2005). Nord and Jermier (1994) conclude that a person may resist change from a healthy sense of psychological protection against the unknown aspects of the proposed change. This is another aspect of resistance to change that must be addressed when seeking to overcome the problem.

According to Gilley et al. (2009), many change initiatives fail because the person leading the change fails to properly motivate and communicate with the organizational employers, thereby facilitating resistance to change and the failure of the initiative. Failure of this sort is also identified by Holt et al. (2009) in the discussion of the failure to properly implement the change, followed by a cycle of failure; the failure is reinforced and perpetuated by further inability to initiate the change successfully. Change initiatives are not necessarily doomed to failure.

Individual involvement throughout the organization affects change. Self-leadership is the ability of an individual to generate the necessary self-motivation and self-direction to achieve goals and is more than just avoiding violations of external standards; it is the internalization of being the decision-maker of the rationale for the standards, thereby having a significant influence on any resistance to change (Neck, 1996). As discussed earlier, individuals within organizations have central roles to play in deciding the issue of resisting change.

A proposed change initiative may be resisted by senior leadership because the change creates an unknown variable or situation, and leadership may prefer to deal with issues that are known quantities (Lane et al., 2013). Resistance is a fundamental issue of any project that must be addressed at the beginning of the project. Failure to gain management support will doom the project to failure (Leflar & Siegel, 2013).

METHODS TO OVERCOME RESISTANCE TO CHANGE

The methods for overcoming resistance to change are varied to allow for the differences in the rationale for resistance. Flexibility is an important aspect of overcoming resistance; organizations are complex, and the methods to address problems must be varied.

Avey et al. (2008) propose that positive emotional feelings and attitudes may well address the issue of resistance to change based on cynicism. Furthermore, a positive psychological capital, mindfulness, and positive mental resources are critical to overcoming the harmful and destructive attitudes associated with resistance to change (Avey et al., 2008). Investing in the necessary resources, such as teams of trusted employees and managers devoted to the change initiative, will help avoid a self-perpetuating cycle of cynicism involving employees and management (Stanley et al., 2005). Also, Holt et al. (2009) recommend approaches like small focus groups in which open dialogue is established (distributing information, but also listening) with particular attention to asking why the change may have failed, but this must be communicated with sincerity, honesty, and commitment to the importance of the change. The free exchange of information will help establish the benefit, need, and importance of the change to all involved (Holt et al., 2009).

Kennedy (2011) proposes an interesting approach to addressing resistance to change in the form of self-improvement on the part of the employees through personal acceptance of responsibility for positive organizational participation. Personal association with an initiative is similar to the proposed risk management self-responsibility approach discussed by Leflar and Siegel (2013). Rochet, Keramidas, and Bout (2008) provide a discussion concerning the value of using an actual crisis as a means to successfully implement change through a systems perspective of opportunity to learn and overcome the resistance to change. After significant crises, such as the terrorist attacks of September 11, 2001, the event led to significant changes in many organizations.

According to Rudes (2007), to achieve the best chance at successfully implementing a change, it is necessary to gain the support and involvement of those individuals operating within the organization between the senior leaders and the lower levels of workers. This middle tier of the employee can balance relationships between the top and bottom of the organization and facilitate a better understanding of the goals of the change and how best to implement the change successfully (Rudes, 2007).

Palmer (2004) recommends the use of a seven-method approach to addressing and preventing resistance to change. The seven elements are leading change, creating a shared need, shaping a vision, mobilizing commitment, monitoring progress, finishing the job, and anchoring the change in systems and structures (Palmer, 2004). These seven approaches are necessarily a firm understanding of systems management and effective project management.

Whereas Lane et al. (2013) and Diamond (1992) indicate that leaders may cause or support the resistance to change of a proposed initiative, Wart (2004) indicated that leaders also have the power and influence to prevent resistance to change and have the ability to self-critique their actions fostering a learning opportunity. Diamond (1992) also indicates that a more socially-minded leader seeks to involve the organization's members, thereby reducing the resistance to change. Blank (1990) concluded with recommendations that will reduce or prevent resistance to change:

- Understanding and identifying the causes for any insecurity in the audience related to the change is necessary to address this common issue connected with resistance to change.
- It is advisable to establish a justification for the proposed change so that the audience clearly understands the reasons and need for the change.
- Identify and work to avoid any personal likes and dislikes (prejudices) that may create opportunities for resistance.
- It is necessary to understand the individual perspectives and beliefs of the people involved in the change initiative to understand the opposition, thereby developing a strategy to combat their reasons for resistance.
- Communication problems – it is necessary to effectively present the proposed change and ensure the audience understands the purpose and what is expected of them. Poor communication is a common reason for resistance.
- There may be multiple or complex causes for resistance to change. Any combination of the above reasons may result in an elaborate reason for resistance. Avoid focusing on only one potential cause and seek to understand the issues fully.

CHANGE FAILURES

While Decker et al. (2012) examined the implementation failure rate of projects and concluded that the failure rate is likely between 50% and approximately 70%, the real issue remains. Why do change initiatives fail?

The reasons for failure are easily associated with failing to follow the advice presented in this book. If a change project has an imperfect vision of the organization's result and value, people will not support the project. If the change plan is not aligned with the organization's goals or is underfunded, it will likely fail. If the change manager fails to provide well-crafted messages to the organization about the change initiative and generate vested interest within the organizational culture, the project will likely fail. Possessing insufficient resources to accomplish the change initiative is one of the most fundamental reasons for failure.

Since people are the drivers of any change, they are also the most critical of resources. Change fatigue is common because managers do not always consider it as an issue in the change process. Managers look at what a worker has "on their plate," and determines the availability of that person for a project. The manager overlooks the mental, emotional, and physical strain placed on a person when working on complex change initiatives. For instance, if a three-people team is developing a change plan to implement a business continuity standard at their organization and there are expectations from some leaders that the project completion date will occur within a year, there is a strong possibility that the team will experience change fatigue.

SUMMARY

The importance of overcoming resistance to change associated with an organizational project, program component, or another change initiative cannot be overstated. The success of a significant project may hang in the balance, and any resistance to the proposed change must be identified and addressed before the actual change implementation. Any change that is identified during the implementation phase of the project will necessitate a resolution. Change is an essential activity within an organization seeking to maintain a competitive edge over other organizations, as well as maintaining the necessary flexibility during emergencies.

Addressing the specifics of overcoming resistance to change should be of great interest to practitioners seeking direct methods to accomplish the desired goal. The practical application of these methods should assist in real-world implementation toward affecting resistance to change. In particular, the disciplines of business, security, emergency, and disaster management will benefit from the knowledge of addressing resistance to change. These disciplines seek improvements in implementing various initiatives aimed at achieving risk management, emergency preparedness, or organizational effectiveness.

Organizational change and any associated resistance are not necessarily constant or uniform in rationale. Resistance may come from various levels of the organization and may be the result of various concerns of organizational members (e.g., Blank, 1990; Agócs, 1997; Lane, McCormack, & Richardson, 2013). Resistance to change may come from institutional resistance to change (Agócs, 1997), poor implementation of the change initiative by the project/program manager (Gilley, Gilley, & McMillan, 2009), from a sense of general organizational uncertainty about the change (Kennedy, 2011), or resistance by senior leadership to avoid the unknown risk of potential opportunity (Lane et al., 2013). Palmer (2004) confirms that change failures are caused by human actions, or lack of action, and not by technical issues. Therefore, resistance to change may occur throughout an organization with the members of the organization at the heart of the issue. General uncertainty about a change initiative may result from cynicism, dubious trust of leadership, and the employee's lack the confidence in each other (Kennedy, 2011).

Stanley, Meyer, and Topolnytsky (2005) identify the difference between skeptical resistance to proposed change (doubt in the project) and cynical resistance to the change (doubt or mistrust in management). According to Gilley et al. (2009), many change initiatives fail because the person leading the change fails to properly motivate and communicate with the organizational employers, thereby facilitating resistance to change and the failure of the initiative. Individual involvement throughout the organization affects change.

Self-leadership is the ability of an individual to generate the necessary self-motivation and self-direction to achieve goals and is more than just avoiding violations of external standards; it is the internalization of being the decision-maker of the rationale for the standards, thereby having a significant influence on any resistance to change (Neck, 1996). Resistance is a fundamental issue of any project that must be addressed at the beginning of the project. Failure to gain management support will doom the project to failure (Leflar & Siegel, 2013).

The methods for overcoming resistance to change are varied to allow for the differences in the rationale for resistance. Flexibility is an important aspect of overcoming resistance; organizations are complex, and the methods to address problems must be varied.

Avey et al. (2008) proposed that positive emotional feelings and attitudes may well address the issue of resistance to change based on cynicism. Investing in the necessary resources, such as teams of trusted employees and managers devoted to the change initiative will aid in avoiding a self-perpetuating cycle of cynicism involving employees and management (Stanley et al., 2005). Also, Holt et al. (2009) recommended approaches like small focus groups in which open dialogue is established (distributing information but also listening) with particular attention to asking why the change may have failed, but this must be communicated with sincerity, honesty, and commitment to the importance of the change. The free exchange of information will help establish the benefit, need, and importance of the change to all involved (Holt et al., 2009).

Kennedy (2011) proposed addressing resistance to change in the form of self-improvement on the part of the employees through personal acceptance of responsibility for positive organizational participation. Personal association with an initiative is similar to the proposed risk management self-responsibility approach discussed by Leflar and Siegel (2013). Rochet, Keramidas, and Bout (2008) discussed the value of using an actual crisis as a means to successfully implement change through a systems perspective of opportunity to learn and overcome the resistance to change.

According to Rudes (2007), to achieve the best chance at success-fully implementing a change, it is necessary to gain the support and involvement of middle management. This middle tier of the employee can balance relationships between the top and bottom of the organiza-tion and facilitate a better understanding of the goals of the change and how best to implement the change successfully (Rudes, 2007). Palmer (2004) recommended the use of a seven-method approach to address-ing and preventing resistance to change. The seven elements are leading change, creating a shared need, shaping a vision, mobilizing commit-ment, monitoring progress, finishing the job, and anchoring the change in systems and structures (Palmer, 2004). These seven approaches are essentially a firm understanding of systems management and effective project management.

If a change project has an imperfect vision of the result and value to the organization, people will not support the project. If the change plan is not aligned with the organization's goals or is underfunded, it is likely to fail. If the change manager fails to provide well-crafted messages to the organ-ization about the change initiative and generate vested interest within the organizational culture, the project will likely fail. Possessing insufficient resources to accomplish the change initiative is one of the most funda-mental reasons for failure. Since people are the drivers of any change, they are also the most critical of resources. Change fatigue is common because managers do not always consider it as an issue in the change process. The manager overlooks the mental, emotional, and physical strain placed on a person when working on complex change initiatives.

REFERENCES

Agócs, C. (1997). Institutionalized resistance to organizational change: Denial, inaction and repression. *Journal of Business Ethics*, 16(9), 917–931.

Avey, J. B., Wernsing, T. S., & Luthans, F. (2008). Can positive employees help positive organizational change? Impact of psychological capital and emotions on relevant attitudes and behaviors. *The Journal of Applied Behavioral Science*, 44(1), 48–70.

Blank, R. E. (1990). Gaining acceptance: The effective presentation of new ideas. *Total Quality Management*, 1(1), 69–73.

Coughlan, D., & Rashford, N. (2006). *Organizational change and strategy: An interlevel dynamics approach*. New York, NY: Routledge.

Decker, P., Durand, R., Mayfield, C. O., McCormack, C., Skinner, D., & Perdue, G. (2012). Predicting implementation failure in organization change. *Journal of Organizational Culture, Communications and Conflict*, 16(2), 29–49.

Diamond, M. A. (1992). Hobbesian and Rousseauian identities: The psychodynamics of organizational leadership and change. *Administration & Society*, 24(3), 267–289.

Gilley, A., Gilley, J. W., & McMillan, H. S. (2009). Organizational change: motivation, communication, and leadership effectiveness. *Performance Improvement Quarterly*, 21(4), 75–94.

Holt, D. T., Dorey, E. L., Bailey, L. C., & Low, B. R. (2009). Recovering when a change initiative stalls. *OD Practitioner*, 41(1), 20–24.

Kennedy, D. (2011). Moving beyond uncertainty: Overcoming our resistance to change. *Leader to Leader*, 62, 17–21.

Lane, K. E., McCormack, T. J., & Richardson, M. D. (2013). Resilient leaders: Essential for organizational innovation. *International Journal of Organizational Innovation*, 6(2), 7–25.

Leflar, J., & Siegel, M. (2013). *Organizational resilience: Managing the risks of disruptive events – a practitioner's guide*. Boca Raton, FL: CRC Press.

Neck, C. P. (1996). Thought self-leadership: A self-regulatory approach towards overcoming resistance to organizational change. *International Journal of Organizational Analysis (1993 - 2002)*, 4(2), 202.

Nord, W. R., Jermier, J. M. (1994). Overcoming resistance to resistance: Insights from a study of the shadows. *Public Administration Quarterly*, 17(4), 396.

Palmer, B. (2004). Overcoming resistance to change. *Quality Progress*, 37(4), 35–39.

Rochet, C., Keramidas, O., & Bout, L. (2008). Crisis as change strategy in public organizations. *International Review of Administrative Sciences*, 74(1), 65–77.

Rudes, D. (2007, January). Tied response to organizational change. [Paper presentation]. American Sociological Association, New York, NY, United States.

Stanley, D. J., Meyer, J. P., & Topolnytsky, L. (2005). Employee cynicism and resistance to organizational change. *Journal of Business & Psychology*, 19(4), 429–459.

Wart, M. (2004). A comprehensive model of organizational leadership: The leadership action cycle. *International Journal of Organization Theory and Behavior*, 7(2), 173–208.

CHAPTER EXERCISES

1. **Instilling Risk Management within the Corporate Culture**

   Angelique has been assigned to enhance the organizational resilience of her company. She decides to begin by creating a culture of risk management at the firm. Since she studied change management at school, she has a good idea of where to begin building employee interest and engagement. How do you think Angelique should begin developing an employee culture of risk management involvement and responsibility?

2. **Engaging Employees**

   Aziz works in the facilities management department of his company. His job is to work around and look for facilities-related problems each morning. His goal is to get a jump on any problems before they become severe and contribute to an accident. Aziz wants to be more efficient in his job. He wants to involve the employees on his regular route of the building. From a change management perspective, how should Aziz engage the employees so that the goal of involvement and increased reporting of problems occurs?

Part 2

4

Leadership Involvement
Change Leadership

LEARNING OBJECTIVES

The learning objectives of this chapter are:

- The Differences between Leaders and Managers
- Leadership Approaches and Styles
- Leadership and Organizational Development
- Motivation to Change

While leaders can manage their respective organizations, it is unreasonable to assume that all leaders can perform as change practitioners simply because they are in leadership positions. Being a leader does not necessarily make one an organizational development practitioner. However, a leader can learn to become a change practitioner. Before discussing the leader as a change manager, it is necessary to understand more about the role and expectations of a manager – leader. While there is a distinction between a manager and a leader, there are instances in this book where they will be treated the same. The treatment is one of convenience in discussing the more significant issues of leadership theory.

THE DIFFERENCES BETWEEN LEADERS AND MANAGERS

A change practitioner can be a leader, a manager, or a subordinate within the organization. Understanding the role of a change practitioner requires an understanding of the differences between a leader and a manager. There are noticeable differences when viewing an organization. The traditional view is that a leader holds a higher position within the organization, and a manager is often middle management and below. There are situations where a role is named a manager and is considered a senior leader. What makes a manager, and what makes a leader? A manager is responsible for planning, directing, organizing, and controlling the tactical functions of a business unit. Managers focus on the tactical aspects of an organization; managers make sure the work is completed. The traditional view of leaders involves strategic level activities like visionary development and motivation. Figure 4.1 indicates the traditional view of leaders and managers. However, there is considerable overlap between the practical activities of leaders and managers.

Mintzberg (2011) indicated that there are conceptual differences between a leader and a manager but questioned the practical difference. In practice, the difference between leaders and managers is not only blurred; the difference is, in practical terms, reasonably inconsequential. A leader provides vision and motivation to accomplish goals, but so do managers. Managers are often considered the people responsible for the accomplishment of technical functions within an organization; managers control and direct the staff to accomplish tasks, managers address various labor issues associated with the employees, and ensure the department goals are aligned with the organizational strategic goals. Figure 4.1 indicated the relationship between leaders, managers, and change practitioners. While each large zone reflects the primary functional responsibilities and duties of a role, there is a reasonable degree of overlap where two roles interact. The desired role section of the Venn diagram is the ideal where a person accomplishes the integration of all three functions; this person has the highest chance of successful change initiatives.

LEADERSHIP QUALITIES – APPROACHES

There are a variety of leadership qualities with similarities and differences. During the discussion of qualities and approaches, the leader/manager reference is used to convey the general function of a person

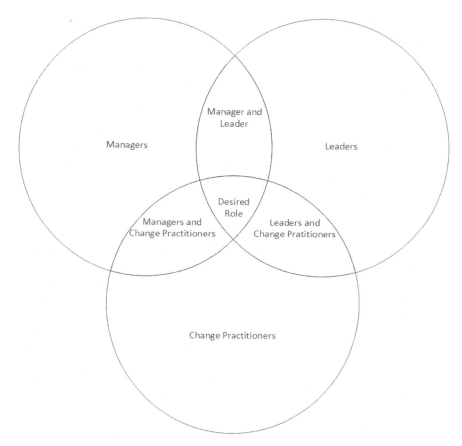

Figure 4.1 Relationship between Leaders, Managers, and Change Practitioners.

in charge of subordinates and responsible for achieving goals. While leaders and managers perform similarly, and at times the same tasks, there is a clear difference between the significant functions performed by each role. The combination of the leader/manager reference is one of convenience.

What makes a great leader or manager? Several descriptions help explain what makes a great leader or manager. The first approach rests with the identification of innate traits or innate qualities and personality characteristics that make a great leader. The traits approach to describing a leader is dependent upon the concept that the leader/manager is born with particular abilities that elevate them to the level of performing as a manager.

The style approach views the leader's behavior as the defining crux of being a manager/leader (Northouse, 2012). Viewing the behaviors instead of traits is more valuable as a learning tool when observing a leader or manager. Behaviors are easily viewed and identified, allowing a subordinate to understand the manager. When considering the style approach, it is advisable to view task behaviors and interpersonal or related tasks. These are self-explanatory and address the behaviors of doing things associated with things and the behaviors of interacting with people.

The skills approach considers the personal capabilities or skills generally grouped as human, technical, and conceptual capabilities (Northouse, 2012). A significant difference between these approaches lies in the concept of a leader born with certain traits and a leader who can learn the skills necessary for being a leader. Learning skills seem more reasonable and current in the way modern thought describes the nature of management.

The situational approach emphasizes the need for the leader to alter the individual style of the leadership to match the situation (Northouse, 2012). While the previous approaches are powerful and useful, the situational approach is more problematic because not all leaders can change their leadership style to match the situation. While the contingency theory matches the leader to the situation, the path–goal theory of leadership proposes to motivate subordinates to achieve the desired goal (Northouse, 2012). Again, matching the manager/leader to the role is a difficult task and often time-consuming.

Finally, there are transformational leaders, servant leaders, and authentic leaders with focuses on providing a charismatic approach to delivering a visionary message to the followers to achieve an organizational goal, providing for the primary benefit of the follower instead of the leader, and communicating an authentic message to the followers that are obvious and real in its approach to leadership (Northouse, 2012). Transformational leadership involves a leader concerned with individual and group influence, emotions, ethical standards, and the importance of each person in the organization (Northouse, 2012). A transformational leader is focused on the development and well-being of subordinates.

A servant leader is similar to a transformational leader in that the well-being of the subordinate is of great value to the leader. Helping the subordinate develop and benefit from their mutual interaction is critical to the servant leader. Transformational, servant, and authentic leaders have a natural style of charisma that allows them to interact on a personal level with subordinates. The leader's actions are influential because they are well-intentioned and focused on the subordinates. Leadership is a form of giving back what is recognized as genuine care of the subordinate, not the leader.

Authentic leaders are viewed from several perspectives that make them difficult to define (Northouse, 2012). The definitions focus on intrapersonal perspectives (i.e., the positive development of the leader), interpersonal perspectives (i.e., the interrelational development of the leader through positive interactions with subordinates), and developmental experiences in the life of the leader resulting in genuine intentions and focus on subordinates because of high ethical standards and compassion (Northouse, 2012).

Leaders embrace a personal approach to leadership that works for them, or at least is comfortable for them to use. As noted above, these approaches are very distinct from one another. They are successful according to the situational constraints surrounding the leader and the leadership environment (Levy, Parco & Blass, 2009). For instance, one highly successful leader may not be successful in a different environment or situation; leaders are not trained for every issue, and that includes being a change management practitioner. There are many different leadership approaches, and the effectiveness of an approach depends on the individual leader as well as the environment in which the leader operates. For instance, an authoritarian leader may be highly successful in a situation where the completion of a project relies on completing numerous tasks according to ordinal and time constraints. However, that authoritarian leader may find it extremely challenging in a role that requires diplomacy and worker involvement in decision making. Not all leaders are the same, just as situations and environments differ.

LEADERSHIP AND ORGANIZATIONAL DEVELOPMENT

Organizational development practitioners must be well versed in understanding the systems dynamics of organizations and the complexities of change within an organization, and this is not common knowledge. It is unreasonable to assume that all leaders would be capable of performing the functions of an OD practitioner. A key component of organizational development is an understanding of the complexities and dynamics of systems thinking. Systems thinking explains the interdependencies and complexities of an organization (Gharajedaghi, 2011). A leader may learn to become an OD practitioner, but it does require formal education and training.

Church, Waclawski, and Burke (1996) discussed the degree of knowledge OD practitioners have concerning the management of organizational change. The data indicated that most OD practitioners were transformational leaders when managing change initiatives due to experiential knowledge, professional training, and formal advanced education (Church, Waclawski, & Burke, 1996). The specialized training and education associated with organizational development (i.e., change management) provide the necessary abilities; generic leaders do not necessarily have this knowledge, and often only receive business administration education.

OD practitioners possessing the necessarily advanced education in conducting change initiatives have a significantly better opportunity to manage change than leaders, managers, and executives lacking the OD knowledge (Burke, Church, & Waclawski, 1993). There is a clear indication that specialized training, education, and experiential knowledge are needed to manage change initiatives. Managers are good at managing their organizations, but OD practitioners are better at managing the issues associated with change management.

OD PRACTITIONERS AND MOTIVATION TO CHANGE

Organizational change is a fundamental component of organizational development; effecting change in an organization is complex and challenging. Organizational culture is the foundation of an organization (Frame, 2013), and any change initiative must consider the culture to be successful. Instilling the motivation and commitment to change within an organization involves more than just requiring the employees to follow the lead of the leader. The culture of the organization is both formal and informal, and influences change within an organization. Recognizing and understanding the culture is a critical issue in establishing motivation and commitment within the employee population.

Senge (2006) presents an excellent method to instill motivation and commitment to change through the development of a shared vision. Having the employees buy into a change is not a new idea; developing a shared vision is much more than acceptance of a change. A shared vision is the transition of a personal vision to a shared vision among the organizational members (Senge, 2006). Attempting to implement a change initiative through the sole involvement of leadership is both challenging and likely to fail because the employees do not have a vested interest in the change. Involving the employees at the earliest stage of a project is an excellent way to develop motivation and commitment. Involving the employees early in the change process is a powerful message to the employees that their involvement is critical to the organization.

The establishment of a shared vision is a process of bringing different personal approaches together through active participant involvement and the blending of many visions into a single shared vision (Senge, 2006). Organizational learning is an integral part of instilling the concept of acceptable change involvement in an organization (Coughlan, & Rashford, 2006). Involving the employees as partners in establishing and maintaining the welfare of the organization is an excellent method of establishing high motivation and commitment to change.

MYER–BRIGGS TYPE INDICATOR ASSESSMENTS

The Myer–Briggs Type Indicator (MBTI) grew out of Jung's work on personality. The personality indicator assessment that is used today is useful in understanding a person's type of personality. While the purpose of this book is other than detailing the MBTI, there is value in providing general information to allow the reader to explore the MBTI in more detail. Excellent information about the MBTI is available at the Foundation web page (myersbriggs.org). There are other web pages with useful information about personality types such as (16personalities.com/), which allows users to participate in a free personality assessment. The personality-type assessment might help you understand more about yourself and others. Consider the possibilities of understanding why people do certain things and how to approach them for better results in professional situations.

Author's Note: I took the assessment several times, and I am an ISTJ (i.e., Introverted, Observant, Thinking, and Judging). The ISTJ determination is very accurate, which is why I have a burning desire to bring order to chaos. While I fit into the ISTJ type nicely, I even carried the nickname of Mr. Spock at one time. However, I also show tendencies that are outside of the ISTJ personality type. I am flexible when interacting with other people to accomplish goals and brainstorming. I love to discuss the possibility of "what if" – I suppose that explains my love of change management. My interest in change management is involved. I am traditional in many ways, but I love to develop and implement change when there is a need. Once I see the benefits of a change initiative, I am committed to the change. If I do not see the value or dislike the logical underpinnings, I will attempt to negotiate a change to improve the concept. I view the personality types as guides to help you understand why you are the way you are, but remember, it is a guide and not an absolute stamp. We are complex beings – we are humans.

SUMMARY

Mintzberg (2011) indicated that there are conceptual differences between a leader and a manager but questioned the practical difference. In practice, the difference between leaders and managers is not only blurred; the difference is, in practical terms, reasonably inconsequential. A leader provides vision and motivation to accomplish goals, but so do managers. Managers are often considered the people responsible for the accomplishment of technical functions within an organization; managers control and direct the staff to accomplish tasks, managers address various labor issues associated with the employees, and ensure the department goals are aligned with the organizational strategic goals.

While leaders and managers perform similarly, and at times the same tasks, there is a clear difference between the significant functions performed by each role. The combination of the leader/manager reference is one of convenience and perhaps even necessary. Several descriptions help explain what makes a great leader or manager.

The traits approach rests with the identification of innate traits or innate qualities and personality characteristics that make a great leader. The style approach views the leader's behavior as the defining crux of being a manager/leader (Northouse, 2012). The skills approach considers the personal capabilities or skills generally grouped as human, technical, and conceptual capabilities (Northouse, 2012). The situational approach emphasizes the need for the leader to alter the individual style of the leadership to match the situation (Northouse, 2012). While the contingency theory matches the leader to the situation, the path–goal theory of leadership proposes to motivate subordinates to achieve the desired goal (Northouse, 2012). Finally, there are transformational leaders, servant leaders, and authentic leaders with focuses on providing a charismatic approach to delivering a visionary message to the followers to achieve an organizational goal, providing for the primary benefit of the follower instead of the leader, and communicating an authentic message to the followers that are obvious and real in its approach to leadership (Northouse, 2012).

Transformational leadership involves a leader concerned with individual and group influence, emotions, ethical standards, and the importance of each person in the organizations (Northouse, 2012). A servant leader is similar to a transformational leader in that the well-being of the subordinate is of great value to the leader. Transformational, servant, and authentic leaders have a natural style of charisma that allows them to interact on a personal level with subordinates. Authentic leaders are viewed from several perspectives that make them difficult to define (Northouse, 2012). The definitions focus on intrapersonal perspectives (i.e., the positive development of the leader), interpersonal perspectives (i.e., the interrelational development of the leader through positive interactions with subordinates), and developmental experiences in the life of the leader resulting in genuine intentions and focus on subordinates because of high ethical standards and compassion (Northouse, 2012).

While leaders are capable of managing their respective organizations, it is unreasonable to assume that all leaders are capable of performing as OD or change practitioners simply because they are in leadership positions. Being a leader does not necessarily make one an organizational development practitioner. However, a leader can learn to become an OD practitioner. Organizational development practitioners must be well versed in understanding the systems dynamics of organizations and the complexities of change within an organization, and this is not common knowledge.

OD practitioners possessing the necessarily advanced education in conducting change initiatives have a significantly better opportunity to manage change than leaders, managers, and executives lacking the OD knowledge (Burke, Church, & Waclawski, 1993). There is a clear indication that specialized training, education, and experiential knowledge are needed to manage change initiatives. Managers are good at managing their organizations, but OD practitioners are better at managing the issues associated with change management.

Organizational culture is the foundation of an organization (Frame, 2013), and any change initiative must consider the culture to be successful. Instilling the motivation and commitment to change within an organization involves more than just requiring the employees to follow the lead of the leader. The culture of the organization is both formal and informal and influences change within an organization. Recognizing and understanding the culture is a critical issue in establishing motivation and commitment within the employee population.

Senge (2006) presents an excellent method to instill motivation and commitment to change through the development of a shared vision. A shared vision is the transition of a personal vision to a shared vision among the organizational members (Senge, 2006). Attempting to implement a change initiative through the sole involvement of leadership is both challenging and likely to fail because the employees do not have a vested interest in the change. Involving the employees at the earliest stage of a project is an excellent way to develop motivation and commitment.

Involving the employees early in the change process is a powerful message to the employees that their involvement is critical to the organization. Organizational learning is an integral part of instilling the concept of acceptable change involvement in an organization (Coughlan, & Rashford, 2006). Involving the employees as partners in establishing and maintaining the welfare of the organization is an excellent method of establishing high motivation and commitment to change.

REFERENCES

Burke, W., Church, A., & Waclawski, J. (1993). What do OD practitioners know about managing change? *Leadership & Organization Development Journal, 14*(6), 3–11.

Church, A., Waclawski, J., & Burke, W. (1996). OD practitioners as facilitators of change: An analysis of survey results. *Group & Organization Studies (1986–1998), 21*(1), 22–67.

Coughlan, D. & Rashford, N. (2006). *Organizational change and strategy: An interlevel dynamics approach.* New York, NY: Routledge.

Frame, J. D. (2013). *Framing decision: Decision making that accounts for irrationality, people, and constraints.* San Francisco, CA: Jossey-Bass.

Gharajedaghi, J. (2011). *Systems thinking: Managing chaos and complexity: A platform for designing business architecture.* (3rd ed.). New York, NY: Elsevier.

Levy, D., Parco, J. & Blass, F. (2009). *The 52nd floor: Thinking deeply about leadership.* Montgomery, AL: Enzo Books.

Mintzberg, H. (2011). *Managing.* San Francisco, CA: Barrett-Koehler.

Northouse, P. G. (2012). *Leadership: Theory and practice.* (6th ed.). Thousand Oaks, CA: Sage.

Senge, P. (2006). *The fifth discipline: The art and practice of the learning organization.* New York, NY: Doubleday.

CHAPTER EXERCISES

1. **Planning a New Change Initiative**
   Your manager has tasked you with developing a plan to develop a crisis management program at your company. You are well versed in crisis management but new to change management. You contact someone in strategic planning that studied organizational development and change. In a brief exchange of emails, your "expert" advises you to learn about the organization. What do you think he meant?

2. **Team Building**
   You are a physical security director tasked with implementing a video surveillance system for the corporate HQ. You want to make sure that the project is a success. You have been advised to identify key personnel to help ensure the change initiative is successful. The most experienced employees are involved in several significant projects. Who do you think should be involved in the project team?

3. **Physical Security: Workplace Violence/General Security**
   As the security manager for a large company, you responsible for improving the physical security of the principal corporate office. The senior leaders have become concerned with workplace violence, and your supervisor has requested a plan to enhance the security of the facility. What are the high-level change issues associated with the project?

5

Practical Organizational Considerations

LEARNING OBJECTIVES

The learning objectives of this chapter are:

- Critical Variables in Organizational Transformation
- Organizational Structures and the Impact of Politics
- Leadership, Performance, and Culture
- The Complexities of Change Management and Organizational Theory

Several organizational components affect change initiatives and transformations because of their critical influence throughout the organization. The components are Human Resource (HR) policies, internal and external stakeholders, and the organizational culture. The holistic nature of an organization is dependent upon the employees that develop goals, perform the processes of achieving goals, as well as creating culture. The people associated with an organization include more than just internal employees; the external people involved with an organization are often critical to the success of the organization. The development of a transformation effort that involves the entire organization requires careful and comprehensive planning and involvement of the organization to realize success. The key variables are organizational structure, human resource policies, leadership and trust, and performance measures.

CRITICAL VARIABLES IN ORGANIZATIONAL TRANSFORMATION

A large-scale organizational transformation affects the entire organization, and several vital variables should be considered to ensure the most excellent chance of success in implementing the change. The key variables are organizational structure, Human Resource policies, leadership and trust, and performance measures. The organizational structure reflects the established authority relationships, and any associated diagram illustrates how the organization chart is aligned for business performance. Human Resource policies are the rules by which the organization operates from both an operational and administrative perspective. The policies provide the guidelines through which people are compensated, rewarded, and told how to behave while at work.

In some cases, the policies may also include requirements as to how an employee must behave outside of work. The leadership of an organization provides management, vision, and establishes the reasons why things are done. The leadership leads the organization; without the explicit and reasoned leadership, the organization is lost. Also, the trust aspect of leadership must be without question. If the workers cannot trust the leaders, there will likely be a severe problem between employees and management; the lack of trust will lead to little effort on the part of the workers. Performance measures allow an organization to understand how well goals are accomplished according to established criteria. Establishing the criteria to assess the performance of individuals, groups, and significant parts of the organization allows the company to determine the effectiveness and act accordingly to continue to achieve goals as planned or modify plans to become more efficient.

ORGANIZATION STRUCTURE

The organizational structure is a description of the official authority relationships within the organization. The structure of the organization represents the people within the organization. The organizational diagram is representative of the design selected for the organization; a typical design shows the senior leader at the top of the structure and the hierarchical display of the employees below. The diagram identifies the positions of the employees according to the desired presentation approach; some examples of the approaches might be functional, geographic, or product. The

74

structure of the organization, as described in a diagram, represents the official or formal relationships. However, there are also informal relationships within the organization that may not match the structural diagram. The informal relationships reflect personal and professional friendships that influence the organization; these relationships are not a function of the structure but may have a tremendous impact on processes. The informal nature of relationships will affect operational processes. The processes are expected to follow a particular flow according to the organizational structure but may follow a very different workflow. Planning for transformational change should consider both the official and unofficial structures of the organization.

The functional, geographic, or product approaches to designing the organization are practical issues that must be understood during the development of a change initiative. The functional design groups the workers according to their job function. For instance, the security department contains the security employees, and the finance department consists of the finance employees. The geographic design represents the organization according to the location within a state, country, or region of the world. The geographic design often indicates the decentralization of job functions. The product design is similar to the geographic, except the design is based on the product or service created for the organization. The decentralized product and geographic approaches reflect the specific purpose of the structural design. However, there is also the possibility that the organizational design is a hybrid of one of these designs. A hybrid design takes the best parts of various designs and incorporates them into a design that benefits the organization; following hard-set rules about design is the antithesis of a supportive and effective organizational design. The design of the organization should match the most efficient reflection of the organizational accomplishment of business goals and strategies. Transformational change must account for the best design possible and acknowledge the importance of following the approved synergistic design.

THE IMPACT OF POLICIES

The policies of the HR Department reflect the expectations of acceptable behavior along with the rules associated with rewards, benefits, and punishments. The HR policies influence the organization and should be developed with care. Increased organizational performance is linked to the HR policies and programs of an organization (Besma, 2014). The HR handbook is an artificial attempt at documenting the rules of the workplace society. The employees must be able to understand and view the workplace society standards, mores, guidelines, and control mechanisms that allow the organization to function effectively. For example, the policy on vacations indicates the accrual rate per a given period (e.g., month) and how much many hours or days of accrued time may be saved. It is wise to limit the amount of time an employee can save to avoid the accrual of large quantities of time; the accrual of a significant amount of vacation time is equal to the amount of money represented by that time – time equals money. The HR Handbook contains the collected rules of behavior, the policies surrounding benefits, and general employment; some employees may have contracts with employment conditions that are different from the typical Handbook conditions.

A planned transformational change must accommodate and reflect the rules within the HR policies; the HR policies bring structure to the organization. Otherwise, there would be chaos created by people acting as they please. All changes must conform to the constraints and rules of the organization so that the cultural fabric is not destroyed; parity within an organization is essential – everyone must feel comfortable and consider the treatment as fair.

LEADERSHIP INTERACTION

The leaders of an organization are highly influential in the transformational process. All change initiatives require the full support of senior leadership to increase the chance of success. However, the quality of the support influences more than just the change effort. The effect of leadership communication within the organization can make the difference between success and failure. Leaders communicating through active and supportive messages about the transformation, in conjunction with sincere and honest messages about the initiative, and the full support of the leaders to promote the change will likely result in success (Gilley, Gilley, & McMillan, 2009).

Organizational leadership plays a significant role in reducing the resistance to change and can be impactful at various levels of the organization (Blank, 1990; Agócs 1997; Lane, McCormack, & Richardson, 2013). The leaders of the organization may influence the transformational change by failing to provide their full support because of personal resistance to the initiative caused by uncertainty and fear of the unknown risk associated with the effort (Lane et al., 2013). Failures in leadership during transformational change initiatives are viewable in organizational cynicism, lack of trust in the leaders, and the employees experiencing a lack of confidence in one another (Kennedy, 2011).

The leaders of the organization wield considerable influence and control within the organization. The delivery of an honest, sincere, and personal message from the leaders to the employees about a change can make the difference and foster success. The reduction in resistance is imperative, and a leader can garner holistic support through effective communication throughout the organization.

PERFORMANCE MEASURES

Typical organizational performance metrics focus on financial measurements related to expense and return on investment. Besma (2014) suggests that the costs associated with the operation of the HR Department are not operational expenses, but rather capital investments that support the well-being of the organization. The metrics that are measuring characteristics of the organizational operation should be considered carefully to ensure they capture the necessary data for the appropriate goal. The example of Michael Eisner identifying the number of movies made in a fiscal year affecting the success of the Disney amusement parks is an essential lesson in understanding the organizational goals and how best to measure them (Cameron & Quinn, 2011). Organizations compete for business, and ensuring the organizational concept of operation is aligned correctly for success will result in an efficient or dysfunctional organization (Cameron & Quinn, 2011).

Xenikou & Simosi (2006) suggest that the positive social environment of the workplace results in positive organizational performance. The measurement of data is more complicated than the collection of a number relating to the sale of a particular object. Quantitative data is one type of data collection; qualitative data may provide robust information about processes and achieving goals. For instance, a business that focuses on making people happy is interested in the level of happiness and the number of individuals purchasing services. The level of happiness may translate into repeat business or recommendations to friends and family.

The type of leadership associated with a transformation has profound influence within the organization. Hu, Gu, & Chen (2013) indicate that organizational transformation resulting in innovative results are related to transformational leadership. The innovative results of transformational

77

leadership will also influence the performance results of the organization. Applying an integrative approach to HR policies will lead to increased performance results (Dobre, 2012). Both leadership and HR policies are the means through which an organization operates with a clear vision, direction, and rewards leading to high levels of performance.

PEOPLE, POLICIES, AND CULTURE IN ORGANIZATIONAL TRANSFORMATIONS

People are the fundamental component of an organization and the primary element in organizational transformations. Everything about the organization is associated with the people that develop goals, perform the processes of achieving goals, as well as providing the basis for the culture. The people related to an organization include more than just internal employees; the external people involved with an organization are often critical to the success of the organization.

Planned change initiatives seeking to effect improvements at an organization should include both internal and external stakeholders to ensure the full organization. Human Resource policies should be acknowledged as affecting change initiatives both as a result of change and as a catalyst for change. Also, the organizational culture must be considered in any transformation effort because of the power, both formal and informal, that the cultural aspects have within the organization. The Competing Values Framework (Cameron & Quinn, 2011) evaluates the organizational components. The Framework provides a meaningful explanation of the interaction of each topical area from an organizational perspective.

COMPETING VALUES FRAMEWORK

The Competing Values Framework model is based on the research discussed in Cameron and Quinn (2011) as two primary dimensions of successful organizations. These dimensions focus on stability and control and internal integration versus external differentiation. The four quadrants of the matrix reflect the different types of organizational approaches to conducting business. The approaches are very different from one another and involve fundamentally opposing philosophies to conducting business. The opposing values of these approaches can be seen in the different values – control versus stability and internal versus external

(Cameron & Quinn, 2011). Four culture profiles illustrate the major organizational groupings. Each of the four styles produces successful organizations, given the right conditions.

FOUR MAJOR CULTURE PROFILES

The Competing Values Framework, as described by Cameron and Quinn (2011), consists of four major culture profiles: Clan (collaborative), Adhocracy (creative), Hierarchy (control), and Market (competition). Cameron and Quinn (2011) present the two by two matrixes as relationships that are not necessarily precise, but rather continuum-based cultural intersections. Each approach will produce a fruitful and efficient organization, but one approach is not inherently better than the others; the organization determines the most appropriate approach to achieving success. It is essential to understand the culture of an organization when considering change management. The culture of the organization will influence the types of changes, approaches to change, and outcome expectations.

INTERNAL AND EXTERNAL STAKEHOLDERS

All organizations consist of internal and external stakeholders (i.e., people involved with the organization). The internal stakeholders are typically easy to identify because they are involved and identified within organizational operations. Internal stakeholders range from the senior-most level of management (e.g., the Board of Directors) down to the new intern working on a summer project.

The external stakeholders are harder to identify because of the complexity of organizations and the critical nature of supply chains. External stakeholders may range from all the companies and the associated personnel that provide devices, components, or supplies to the subject organization, to all of the people that provide tangential services that are of value to the organization. The broad reference to tangential services is necessary because the limits of external stakeholders are as wide or narrow as the desired definition. For instance, a software vendor that provides critical software to perform accounting or project management services is an external stakeholder.

The Competing Values Framework views stakeholders are natural sources of significant interaction with the organization. For instance, the customer is a critical external stakeholder in each profile because the client is the user of the service or product from the organization. The grounding of the adhocracy culture in creative activities and the external user (customer) as the primary focus of the organization, results in effective products designed to capture the imagination; the customer must love the product for the adhocracy culture to achieve success.

ORGANIZATIONAL COMMUNITY

The HR Department recruits and provides services to the employees of an organization. HR touches every employee from the top-down and is expected to provide fair, consistent policies designed to ensure the efficient operation of the organization. Achieving organizational goals relies on policy development surrounding the behavior and compensation of the employees. The policies attempt to establish the necessary constraints on behavior, like a society establishing controls on behavior, and these control limitations are associated with the culture of the organization. The members of the organization constitute a subset of the larger external society. Each organization has a particular society with norms of behavior. For instance, the attire of the employees is a common issue of concern; some companies allow any attire, and other companies have rigid rules on acceptable clothing to include the color of a business suit.

Cameron and Quinn (2011) indicate the fundamental differences between the four cultural profiles from an HR perspective. The clan culture produces the HR function as the champion of the workers; the adhocracy culture sees the HR role as a change agent within the organization; hierarchy culture produces the HR specialist seeking efficiency, and the marker culture reveals HR as a business partner (Cameron & Quinn, 2011). The differences between these roles indicate that the HR function is not static, but changeable according to the philosophical and cultural approach of the organization.

The policies developed by HR are not arbitrary or capricious; they reflect the culture or profile of the organization. Creative organizations have greater internal flexibility allowing the employees to achieve higher levels of creativity. Hierarchical cultures are more rigid and demanding adherence to protocols. A clan organization is more collaborative within the employee approach to achieving goals and therefore focused on the commitment and development of the employee. For instance, developing an employee is essential, and the organization is likely to have professional and personal development programs such as tuition assistance. The market profile can be seen in financial organizations where commission employees receive high commissions for achieving sales and profits goals. This type of organization probably has an experienced security and risk management operation to detect fraud; fraud is a common risk in commission-based operations.

ORGANIZATIONAL CULTURE

The culture of an organization consists of various principles, traditions, beliefs, and philosophical approaches to conducting business. The culture represents the people (i.e., employees and stakeholders) and their respective formal and informal attitudes toward achieving organizational objectives. The culture is more than just attitudes; it is the fundamental fabric of the organization and the organizational soul. The Competing Values Framework indicates that each organization has a distinct culture associated with the approach to achieving organizational objectives or efficiency (Cameron & Quinn, 2011).

The clan culture focuses on collaboration and balanced relationships between the internal integrative elements of business and the discretionary approaches to business. The adhocracy or creative culture concentrates on the external delivery of achievements; there is considerable flexibility in the approach to achieving goals; the creative mind needs more freedom to excel. The hierarchical or control-oriented culture is much more traditional. It flourishes in a stable organization that exhibits control over the elements of the organization. The culture appears as a rather inflexible approach to discretion; these are the old businesses like IBM and big banks. Market-driven cultures focus on competition through a controlled internal environment and a highly flexible external environment; achieving the sales objectives requires flexible external decision-making.

THE COMPLEXITIES OF CHANGE MANAGEMENT

Organizations are varied in size, purpose, and fundamental design. However, they have similarities in that each organization has a purpose, and it has employees. Researchers look at how people form groups, perform their work, react to a stimulus, and draw conclusions from the data. Organizational research helps academics and practitioners to understand the complexities within the internal and external environment of an organization. It is essential for practitioners operating within the organizational arena to understand how and why theory, change agents, and employees affect both non-profit and for-profit organizations. Researchers provide that knowledge through careful study and theory development.

ORGANIZATIONAL THEORY AND THE REAL WORLD

The age-old question of which came first, theory, or practice is an excellent place to begin the discussion of organizational theory concerning the real world. The "real world" is simply the practice of operating within an actual organization. Practice and theory are different sides of the same coin; they go hand-in-hand and exist in conjunction with one another. Researchers look at actual organizations and the employees as subjects to study to learn more about the dynamics of the organizations. Practitioners use theories about organizations and employees to affect change within an organizational environment. Researchers learn from actual organizations, practitioners learn from research theory and practical experience. Shepherd and Sutcliffe (2011) discussed the deductive nature of operating from a theory to view specifics (top-down theorizing) and the inductive approach of viewing specifics to develop a theory (bottom-up theorizing) as primary ways to view the relationship between theory and real-world practice.

Suddaby, Hardy, and Huy (2011) indicated that much of the theory addressing organizations come from other disciplines such as engineering, sociology, and psychology. Also, most of the theory literature addressing organizations is from the 1960s and the 1970s, not because there is nothing new, but because of the nature of how information is reviewed and presented by academic journals (Suddaby, Hardy, & Huy, 2011). Pryor, Humphreys, Oyler, Taneja, and Toombs (2011) explained theory acceptance as a function of the amount of communication and publication of the theory; primarily, the acceptance and popularity of a theory are based on the marketing of that theory.

ORGANIZATIONAL THEORY AND CHANGE MANAGERS

Change within an organization is often a stress-inducing activity for everyone involved. Those held responsible for implementing change experience stress because they must program or project manages a planned change event that may not be popular. Employees experiencing a planned change must cope with a change they may not like or a change that directly impacts their job. In any case, change is stressful and requires special consideration when being planned. Managers must understand that there may be resistance to change. However, there are methods for addressing the issues associated with change resistance. Holt, Dorey, Bailey, and Low (2009) suggest using small group discussions to open a free-exchange dialogue that focuses on both speaking and listening to identify any reasons for the difficulty. This dialogue will help establish the benefit, need, and importance of the change to all involved (Holt et al., 2009).

Managers are held responsible for the successful operation of organizational units, and this includes successfully developing, implementing, and assessing change within the organization. To ensure success, managers must understand the issues involved in change management. Understanding organization behavior theory, communication theory, and project management theory are critical to personal and organizational success. Change is critical to the survival and resilience of an organization, and managers must be able to engage the workforce to complete a change strategy.

ORGANIZATIONAL THEORY AND EMPLOYEES

Employees are the heart of any organization. Organizations are not static entities; they are ever-changing because the environment in which they exist is ever-changing. People constitute a significant change agent within organizations because they are reacting to changing internal and external organizational issues. Stead (1972) indicates an interesting application of Berlo's communication model concerning management theories and employee involvement. As one person sends a message to another person, there is the possibility of interference occurring during the sending or receiving of the message due to particular management theory approaches affecting how the message is received and interpreted (Stead, 1972). For instance, a Supervisor attempting to change the behavior of an employee sends a Theory Y message; however, the message is received as a Theory X message (Stead, 1972). This communication process was unsuccessful from both the Supervisor's and employee's perspectives requiring an alteration in the message for the successful transmission of the message. The dynamic nature of employee interactions within an organization is challenging and complex for all those involved, which explains why so much effort goes into selecting, developing, and retaining the right employees for an organization.

PUBLIC ORGANIZATIONS AND PRIVATE ORGANIZATIONS

Organizations are not all the same. It is easy to see differences when assessing or categorizing organizations based on criteria such as products, services, purposes, profit, or non-profit. The fundamental difference between public and private organizations is the purpose and goal of the organization (Leflar & Siegel, 2013). A public organization (non-profit, service-oriented) seeks to provide a service or product to the public as part of a governmental or quasi-governmental function without focusing on making a profit. For instance, a city library provides an essential service to the people of the city; the organizational goal is to provide library services to the public. The operation of a public organization by a governmental body or a Board of Directors appointed to facilitate the functioning of the organization is in the interest of the public.

A private organization is profit-driven and responsible to shareholders. The goal of a private organization (business) is to deliver goods or services to customers with the intent to make a profit for the shareholders. For instance, Exxon seeks to make a profit for the shareholders through the sale of petroleum products. The sole purpose of this company is to make a profit for those who have invested in the company (shareholders). The private organization may offer some public service or good that benefits non-shareholders, but the fundamental purpose of the private organization is to provide a profit for the shareholders. Indeed, the workforce at the organization benefits from having a job, but that is a necessity for the operation of the organization. It is very likely that if an organization could operate and make a profit without a workforce, it would because the workforce is an expense for the organization.

ORGANIZATIONAL TRANSFORMATION STRATEGIES

The discussion contained within addresses strategies to achieve organizational transformation. To better understand the component strategies of strategic, incremental, reactive, and anticipatory, the management system used in the ANSI/ASIS Organizational Resilience Management Standard (ASIS ORM.1, 2017) is presented as a robust framework to achieve the goals of developing, implementing, and monitoring the transformative change initiative. The ASIS ORM.1-2017 standard is based on a systems perspective of organizations, uses a Plan-Do-Check-Act cyclical approach to moving from one component to the next, and an iterative process of change to allow for profound and manageable process change (ASIS International, 2017).

STRATEGIC-LEVEL TRANSFORMATIONAL STRATEGY

The strategic-level organizational transformation strategies affect the holistic nature of the organization at all levels. The strategic issues of change focus on organizational structure, policy, governance, and regulatory issues, senior leader support, internal–external environmental concerns, and technology interdependencies (ASIS International, 2017). A fundamental strategic concern is a justification for pursuing the change initiative. For instance, if an organization attempts to achieve an enhanced level of organizational resilience, the goal must be in alignment with the business goals of the organization (Leflar & Siegel, 2013). Organizational leaders have a responsibility to conduct business to benefit the employees and the organizations (Levy, Parco, & Blass, 2009).

A strategic issue is incorporating the change into the governance process, as well as the structural processes of the organization so that it becomes part of the organization; it must become a long-term, sustainable element of the organization (Coughlan, & Rashford, 2006; Galbraith, Downey, & Kates, 2002). The strategic aspects of change require that the senior leadership must actively support the change and maintain the involvement of the internal–external stakeholders of the organization (Coughlan, & Rashford, 2006; Galbraith, Downey, & Kates, 2002). There is another quality or element of the organization that must be fully involved positively; the change initiative must become part of the organizational culture to become a transformational change (Coughlan, & Rashford, 2006). The culture of the organization is a strategic matter because the culture is the root of the organization and carries the values, traditions, formal and informal expectations, and beliefs.

INCREMENTAL-LEVEL TRANSFORMATIONAL STRATEGY

An incremental approach to viewing the process of transformational change is critical in that organizations are complex, and change may take place at different rates; sometimes, the difference in change rate is intentional and designed into the implementation phase. An incremental approach to implementing change to improve organizational resilience is a better method because of the increased control opportunities (Leflar & Siegel, 2013). Also, the iterative nature of the ASIS ORM.1-2017 framework makes incremental change strategies inherent to the management system (ASIS International, 2017). The importance of regular feedback from the organization provides critical information during the process of the change initiative; it provides opportunities for improvement throughout the process (Galbraith, Downey, & Kates, 2002). A powerfully valuable component of incremental change is the ability to assess the plan against the current process and the attainment of the goals; it is acceptable to modify the project work to gain the necessary alignment with the planned goals or adjust the goals if they are flawed (Coughlan & Rashford, 2006). Maintaining the pace of the implementation is essential (i.e., avoid moving too fast or too slow) so that the organization does not lose focus or interest in the change (Galbraith, Downey, & Kates, 2002). A great value to the organization during a change initiative is the very nature of incremental change; the organization can see the change take hold and possibly increase efficiencies or enhance the resilience of the organization.

REACTIVE TRANSFORMATIONAL STRATEGY

Reacting to an event is typical for organizations to identify a reason for a change initiative. In the security field, it is no longer acceptable to have a reactionary approach to addressing risks; waiting until something happens is viewed as unwise and unprepared. There is a logic in taking that perspective, but there are times when reacting to an incident are unavoidable. The ASIS ORM.1-2017 recognizes the reality of reacting to events and seeks to improve the ability of the organization to respond through preparing and anticipating events, thereby preparing the organization for the change of the culture of the organization (ASIS International, 2017). Applying change initiatives to focus on holistic, fundamental issues of the organization allows for the widespread inculcation of accepting personal responsibility for managing the organizational risks (Leflar & Siegel, 2013).

ANTICIPATORY TRANSFORMATIONAL STRATEGY

A significant value of the ASIS ORM.1-2017 standard involves the antici-patory nature of organizational resilience. Organizational resilience con-sists of the adaptive and absorptive capacity of an organization; a critical theoretical component of that is the development of a culture of risk man-agement whereby disruptive acts or unacceptable situations are antic-ipated and addressed (Leflar & Siegel, 2013). Organizational resilience enhancement within an organization is achieved using the ASIS ORM.1-2017, and the anticipatory value of the preparations is one of the most important justifications for the business strategy; the change to enhance resilience relies on prevention and preparedness. Anticipating a situation or threat is based on learning from previous events. The inclusion of many organizational members, along with the open exchange of information, increases organizational learning and allows for the preparation of antici-patory efforts associated with the change initiative (Senge, 2006).

Assessing risks and developing a treatment for the risks that are sup-ported by management is a valuable and potent means of anticipatory strategic thinking that can be built into an organization with little effort. Developing processes that address future events affecting an organization is a simple approach to promoting change management with controlled initiatives that can have transformational effects.

Each of the strategies focuses on a different aspect of change within the broader systems framework; each is important but fundamentally different from the others. The organization is a complicated relationship between various processes, people, and internal–external factors; taking a systems perspective is the best way to understand an organization (Gharajedaghi, 2011).

PROJECT MANAGEMENT VERSUS CHANGE MANAGEMENT

Project managers are excellent at managing the planning, resources, imple-mentation, and documentation associated with a project. However, a pro-ject manager is not necessarily a change management professional. Project managers focus on the project scope and the various project requirements constrained by the budget and time resources for the deliverables. Change managers focus not only on the mechanics of the project too, but also on the people and culture of the organization. While team building is critical for both types of managers, relationship building for change management is from an organizational perspective, depending on the scope of the project. The real difference is the communication and culture awareness aspect of the change manager's focus; how the message about a project is conveyed to the organization is critical to success.

CHANGE CAPACITY

The *change capacity* of a team, group, or organization relates to the ability to perform additional work and provide additional resources for change initiatives. Organizations have a limited supply of resources to implement change – this is a critical concept to understand. Leaders and managers must understand the importance of change capacity. New change initiatives are likely to fail if the organization lacks enough capacity to support the work. Leaders that seek transformative change to remain competitive in the marketplace must plan for the capacity to change; it is a matter of resources such as time, people, money, physical and intellectual assets, and mental energy. The lack of mental and physical energy to participate in a new change project is known as *change fatigue*. People get tired of working on high profile, time-intensive, and demanding projects. Rotating people is an excellent way to allow for recuperation and provide opportunities for other team members to learn new skills.

SUMMARY

Organizations are dynamic, challenging environments that offer many opportunities for researchers and practitioners. Understanding the multidisciplinary nature of organization research and theory development allows for the effective use of valuable knowledge by both researchers and practitioners. The workforce at an organization is the single most valuable resource and challenge for the organization. Understanding the relationship between the organization's design, functionality, and purpose allows for a better understanding of how the people of the organization will facilitate the achievement of the goals of the organization. The goals of a public and private organization may be similar. However, the fundamental purpose (non-profit vs. profit) is different, and the tailored goals to accomplish the essential function of the organization opposite.

Research associated with organization theory is an integral part of understanding the complexities of organizations. Researchers and practitioners learn from the literature produced about relevant topics and drive further knowledge development. It is a cycle of inquiry that is necessary for the ongoing questioning and understanding of organizational dynamics. A practitioner learns about a new concept or approach to facilitating change within an organization allowing for an improvement in the delivery and achievement of goals. Researchers use organizations to look for new insight or the testing of a research question to determine if an approach is practical. It is important to remember that research is not distinct from the real world. An artificial barrier cannot separate theory and practice; they are connected the same way researchers and practitioners are connected. Each relies upon the other for form and substance within a changing environment.

The transformation of an organization may take different approaches. The influence of stakeholders, human resource assets, and the culture of the organization are critical elements that affect any change event. The stakeholders influence the organization internally and externally. The more interrelated and interdependent an organization becomes, the longer the list of people that can influence change. HR is perhaps the single most potent department in an organization; it represents the employees, and the employees drive the organization. The culture permeates the organization like air in a room. The organization is identified according to the culture, but the organization and culture are intertwined as developing entities; it is like the chicken and the egg scenario.

The strategies of strategic, incremental, reactive, and anticipatory were viewed through the management system used in the ASIS ORM.1-2017. The ASIS ORM.1-2017 uses a robust framework to achieve the goals of developing, implementing, and monitoring the transformative change initiative. The transformational goal of enhancing the organizational resilience relies on the strategies discussed herein; the strategies are part of the management system and the fundamental philosophy of organizational resilience. All change initiatives face the potential of resistance; however, there are ways to address the problems, such as communication inhibitors, fear associated with change, and a lack of support from senior management (Gilley, Gilley, & McMillan, 2009).

Key points of interests are the need to include all members of the organization, gain and maintain the active support of senior management, gain the full and active involvement of the organizational culture to achieve the goals, and seek to include cyclical, iterative change processes to maintain control of the quality of the change. A change initiative involves the acknowledgment of the complexities of the organization, and those complexities should be part of the change so that they are not forgotten or poorly addressed.

The change capacity of an organization relates to the ability to perform additional work and provide additional resources for change initiatives. Leaders and managers must understand the importance of change capacity. New change initiatives are likely to fail if the organization lacks enough capacity to support the work. Leaders that seek transformative change to remain competitive in the marketplace must plan for the capacity to change; it is a matter of resources such as time, people, money, physical and intellectual assets, and mental energy. People get tired of working on high profile, time-intensive, and demanding projects. Rotating people is an excellent way to allow for recuperation and provide opportunities for other team members to learn new skills.

REFERENCES

Agócs, C. (1997). Institutionalized resistance to organizational change: Denial, inaction and repression. *Journal of Business Ethics*, 16(9), 917–931.

ASIS International. (2017). *Security and resilience in organizations and their supply chains – Requirements with guidance (ASIS ORM.1-2017)*. Alexandria, VA: American National Standards Institute.

Besma, A. (2014). Strategic human resource management and its impact on organizational performance. *Valahian Journal of Economic Studies*, 5(1), 95–102.

Blank, R. E. (1990). Gaining acceptance: The effective presentation of new ideas. *Total Quality Management*, 1(1), 69–73.

Cameron, K. S., & Quinn, R. E. (2011). *Diagnosing and changing organizational culture: Based on the competing values framework*. (3rd ed.). San Francisco, CA: Jossey-Bass.

Coughlan, D., & Rashford, N. (2006). *Organizational change and strategy: An inter-level dynamics approach*. New York, NY: Routledge.

Dobre, O. I. (2012). The impact of human resource management on organizational performance. *Management Research and Practice*, 4(4), 37–46.

Galbraith, J., Downey, D., & Kates, A. (2002). *Designing dynamic organizations: A hands-on guide for leaders at all levels*. New York, NY: AMACOM.

Gharajedaghi, J. (2011). *Systems thinking: Managing chaos and complexity: A platform for designing business architecture*. (3rd ed.). New York, NY: Elsevier.

Gilley, A., Gilley, J. W., & McMillan, H. S. (2009). Organizational change: motivation, communication, and leadership effectiveness. *Performance Improvement Quarterly*, 21(4), 75–94.

Holt, D. T., Dorey, E. L., Bailey, L. C., & Low, B. R. (2009). Recovering when a change initiative stalls. *OD Practitioner, 41*(1), 20–24.

Hu, H., Gu, Q., & Chen, J. (2013). How and when does transformational leadership affect organizational creativity and innovation? *Nankai Business Review International, 4*(2), 147–166.

Kennedy, D. (2011). Moving beyond uncertainty: Overcoming our resistance to change. *Leader to Leader, 62,* 17–21.

Lane, K. E., McCormack, T. J., & Richardson, M. D. (2013). Resilient leaders: Essential for organizational innovation. *International Journal of Organizational Innovation, 6*(2), 7–25.

Leflar, J., & Siegel, M. (2013). *Organizational resilience: Managing the risks of disruptive events – A practitioner's guide.* Boca Raton, FL: CRC Press.

Levy, D., Parco, J., & Blass, F. (2009). *The 52nd floor: Thinking deeply about leadership.* Montgomery, AL: Enzo Books.

Pryor, M., Humphreys, J. H., Oyler, J., Taneja, S., & Toombs, L. A. (2011). The legitimacy and efficacy of current organizational theory: An analysis. *International Journal of Management, 28*(4), 209–228.

Senge, P. (2006). *The fifth discipline: The art and practice of the learning organization.* New York, NY: Doubleday.

Shepherd, D. A., & Sutcliffe, K. M. (2011). Inductive top-down theorizing: A source of new theories of organization. *Academy of Management Review, 36*(2), 361–380.

Stead, B. (1972). Berlo's communication process model as applied to the behavioral theories of Maslow, Herzberg, and McGregor. *Academy of Management Journal, 15*(3), 389–394.

Suddaby, R., Hardy, C., & Huy, Q. (2011). Where are the new theories of organization? *Academy of Management Review, 36*(2), 236–246.

Xenikou, A., & Simosi, M. (2006). Organizational culture and transformational leadership as predictors of business unit performance. *Journal of Managerial Psychology, 21*(6), 566–579.

CHAPTER EXERCISES

1. Implementing Security Measures

Joe is a security manager in a midsized paper company. He is new to his position; the position is new to the company following an active shooter incident at an adjacent facility. Joe wants to enhance the security of the paper company building and grounds. He has several solid ideas such as electronic access control, surveillance video for the building and the grounds, and photo ID badges tied to the access control system. The security measures are significant change initiatives for the company. How should Joe begin developing his change management approach?

2. **Employee Safety and Change Management**

   Barbara is a senior leader at 123 Corporation, tasked with resolving poor employee attitudes surrounding the performance of a new production project. The previous project manager did not connect with the employees – she was heavy-handed and failed to relate to the employees. There has been an increase in accidents associated with employee concerns. What do you think Barbara should do to address the problems?

Part 3

6

After the Change

LEARNING OBJECTIVES

The learning objectives of this chapter are:

- Maintaining the Change Initiative and Preparing for the Next One
- Technology Changes and Competitive Strategies
- An Industry Change Example
- Personal Change Management

MAINTAINING THE CHANGE INITIATIVE

The period after the focus of the change initiative is critical to future change initiatives. Throughout the initiative, there was considerable marketing and relationship building. All that work has implications beyond the immediate project. The relationships developed during the initiative are precious for future work efforts. It is essential to maintain those relationships and build upon the great work that has been achieved – they are future supporters and champions of your work.

Once a project has reached a point of satisfactory completion, it might become a program requiring ongoing maintenance. Risk-oriented projects often become programs because the risks do not disappear. It is wise to incorporate complex risk issues into long-term assessment efforts. Risk practitioners are continually looking for new risks within an organization; change initiatives follow as a logical approach to resolve problems.

95

PREPARATION FOR THE NEXT CHANGE INITIATIVE

Change initiatives are often part of a department's strategic planning effort. Budgetary concerns and resource allocation determine future projects. For instance, the business continuity 5-year strategic plan allows for department managers to prepare for change initiatives while finishing current projects. It is possible that the same stakeholders will work on multiple projects for over 5 years. Since the same key people might be involved in multiple projects, it is crucial to maintain excellent interpersonal relations. A wise change manager is a people person with an eye to the future.

TECHNOLOGY AS A BUSINESS RISK: TECHNOLOGY CHANGES IMPACTING AN INDUSTRY

It is crucial to consider the concept of change from a broader perspective; it is pervasive and ongoing. While the book has focused on risk practitioners and change initiatives, it is valuable to see how changes in external societal technology impact an industry – the newspaper industry. Consider the changes possible in your discipline. Curry et al. (2015) determined that while social media still requires improvements in privacy, tools, and training, there is great potential for real-time updates during emergencies. Anyone with a smart device has the potential to become an amateur videographer during a crisis, thereby providing immediate updates to the world news agencies and governments.

The technological changes that are occurring in society influence not only the traditional concept of the print format of newspapers, but also the fundamental means of communicating information to society. The discussion addresses strategies promoting competition in the news industry.

INDUSTRY CASE STUDY: NEWSPAPER INDUSTRY AND TECHNOLOGY CHANGES

The industry case study presented is an illustrative discussion and not intended as a comprehensive coverage of the entire newspaper industry. The value of the case study is associated with the historical changes connected to technological innovations and the issues surrounding those changes. Technology is one of the fastest areas of societal change; it is an excellent topic for change managers to consider.

The history of communicating information is the history of human-kind. At first, the routine method of keeping people informed of the events of the day involved word of mouth. Communicating news through a verbal process was the only cost-efficient means of informing a mass population. Only the wealthiest could afford transcribed documents; handwritten documents involved time-consuming calligraphy and were not reasonable for the news of the day. During the early 17th century, the newspaper became a common form of communicating information (Eriksson, Åkesson, and Lund, 2016). As technology changed, the radio became affordable in the early 20th century and challenged the newspaper.

The challenge against newspapers was more than just communicating information to the public; the real challenge involved advertisements (Patch, 1931). Patch (1931) emphasized that the American Newspaper Publishers conducted a study of advertising in 212 surveyed media companies indicating that advertising in newspapers totaled $93.6 million and radio totaled $7.27 million in 1928. In 1930, the total expenditures on newspaper advertisements had dropped to $86 million, and radio advertising had increased to $23.2 million. The competing technologies of print and radio began the ongoing financial challenges facing newspapers.

The communication of news in print form dominated society for hundreds of years, but the issue facing newspapers is not the news or who distributes it to the public. The business income generated by advertisements is the issue facing newspapers. When television became the newest technology competing for advertising funds, newspapers had another source of advertising completion in addition to radio. The same sort of problem occurred when the Internet reached the public. The significant difference between the older media formats and the Internet centers on the level of exposure to society; the Internet is worldwide, and vast numbers of people have access to online sites (Lau & Wydick, 2014). The influence of technology makes a difference when viewing the feasibility of a traditional business, such as a newspaper.

TECHNOLOGICAL CHANGES – THE INTERNET

The incorporation of new technological advances into society may appear to increase with each generation. Moschella (2015) discussed the use of the accepted measurement by economic historians for technology adoption of 50% use in households in the United States. Moschella (2015) emphasized that to reach the 50% use level, the radio took 8 years (1922–1930), the telephone took 26 years (1920–1946), and the black and white television took 9 years (1939–1948). The more modern technology devices such as the personal computer took 17 years (1976–1993); the use of the Internet took 9 years (1993–2002), and between 1980 and 1995, mobile phones took 15 years to achieve the 50% use level (Moschella, 2015). The popularity and growth of companies such as Google, Facebook, and Amazon are not advances in technology, but instead, services that use applications already in use (Moschella, 2015). Moschella (2015) explains that technology advances are not accelerating but diversifying as into by-products of the existing technology foundations (e.g., home robots, smartwatches, and 3D consumer printers). The diversification of technological advances means more opportunities for users to acquire their respective desires (i.e., there are more means of communicating information between people).

The traditional print format of the newspaper industry was limited to growth options in the face of new technology. Between 1950 and 1999, the revenue of the newspaper industry grew at a rate of 7% a year, but between 2000 and 2006, the growth was only 0.35% (Pew Research Center, 2006). As the Internet reached 50% public usage level in 2002 (Moschella, 2015), the revenue generated in the newspaper industry had dropped to 0.35% (Pew Research Center, 2006). Since advertisers seek to promote and sell their product to the public, the radio has inherent advantages over the newspaper, such as frequent commercials and targeted commercial spots. The newspaper is limited to a single-use form of marketing to reach potential customers. The radio also became a free form of communication through handheld devices and vehicles.

COMPETITION STRATEGIES

The newspaper industry must alter the traditional business structure and operational dynamic to remain a viable business interest (Pew Research Center, 2006). While online information services have immediate updates and a variety of distribution outlets, the traditional news media is more professional and established (Pew Research Center, 2006). The reputation of trusted journalism is one of the most significant values associated with newspapers; this is the sort of value to consider when developing competitive strategies. The current online distribution of news is complicated because it is not always clear if the source of the article is reputable. Online news can come from anyone, regardless of professionalism and integrity.

PORTER'S ANALYSIS MODEL

Organizations are complex systems that require in-depth analysis to understand the factors that lead to enhanced performance and profits. Jurevicius (2013) described Porter's value chain analysis (VCA) model as the identification and examination of the internal processes that lead to an understanding of the organizational functions that influence efficiencies and profits. The model consists of analyzing the dichotomy of primary (e.g., incoming supply chain, production, outgoing supply chain, marketing, customer service) and support functions (e.g., human resources, physical infrastructure, technology functions, strategic sourcing) within an organization (Jurevicius, 2013; Grant, 2016).

The primary functions are likely to change according to the type of organization and the specifics of the operation. The support functions may also vary according to the organization. Patterson (1995) described the VCA as a means to separate the components of an organization and identify the critical information that explains the cost or the differentiation of the customer's perspective of value. The importance of the analysis tool rests in the focus of the systemic parts of the organization associated with the product or service (Patterson, 1995). Understanding the system and its parts is necessary during any attempt to understand a product or service.

COMPETITIVE ADVANTAGES

Jurevicius (2013) emphasized that cost and differentiation are the two competitive advantages of the tool leading to strategic development. The cost advantage applies to the cost of making a product or service and focuses on finding efficiencies within the organization to lower cost and increase competitiveness (Jurevicius, 2013). Differentiation involves the development of improved or superior product advantages (Jurevicius, 2013). For instance, a news agency that embraces technology and creates a significant web presence reduces the physical dependence on printing papers and increases access to a broader audience. The larger the audience, the more interest advertisers will take in promoting the news site. The differentiation of sources to communicate the news will increase the benefit to both audience and organization; the greater the benefit, the greater the interest in the site.

The VCA identifies the factors within the organization, explaining the costs of production is vital to understanding how to maximize efficiencies leading to reduced costs. Jurevicius (2013) indicated that the cost advantage approach consists of these five steps:

- Determine the primary and support activities;
- Determine the cost for each activity about the total cost of the product;
- Determine the factors that explain the cost of each activity;
- Determine the interrelatedness or linkages between the activities; and
- Determine ways to reduce costs.

The five steps are standard decision-making approaches to looking at an issue, understanding the full extent of the issue, and seeking opportunities to affect the issue. An analysis of the cost components of a product is useful when attempting to enhance the functions and achieve efficiency, thereby reducing the cost of production.

Decreasing the cost of a product makes the product more attractive to the customer and, therefore, more competitive for the company. Reducing the cost of production will reach a point where quality cannot remain at the current level, and this becomes a strategic issue of quality and cost. If high quality is critical to the success of the product, the cost will have to remain at the tipping point between quality and value. Knowing the point at which quality and cost becomes an issue rests with a thorough analysis of a broad spectrum of the organization. A company can make a strategic decision to maintain high quality and lower the retail price (i.e., reduce profits) in a bid to achieve a competitive advantage.

The Porter tool allows for another necessary type of analysis. The determination of the differentiation advantage of the product is just as crucial in viewing the full spectrum of the product as the cost. According to Jurevicius (2013), the three differentiation advantage steps consist of determining the activities that the customers view as value-adds, determine and evaluate the approaches that lead to enhancing customer value in the product; and determine the optimally sustainable differentiation. The differentiation advantage approach is another practical method for assessing the value of a company's product or service. The differentiation analysis focuses on the unique qualities of a product that are valuable to the consumer, the things the customer views as separating the product from other products on a value scale. Any analysis involving customer opinions of value is likely going to require frequent checks because of the fickle nature of people and trends.

INTERNAL FOCUS

When seeking to understand the advantages an organization has on the market, it is logical to focus on internal issues such as the primary functions of the VCA model. Grant (2016) indicated that the primary activities are the direct production functions, but the secondary activities are equally important. Both the cost advantage and differentiation advantage are ways to analyze relevant components of a company to understand different aspects of the production cycle. It is a common organizational goal to develop cost efficiencies in producing an item. However, the cost is only one side of the production dynamic.

Understanding how the customer views the product is critical to success. Developing a strategy for enhancing the competitive advantage associated with a product must rely on the synergy of the aligned strategic goals and the business unit goals. The internal components of the company are essential to understanding competitive advantage. However, external relationships are just as valuable and may contain hidden concerns.

EXTERNAL CRITICALITIES

Organizations are complex systems that operate on both the internal and external levels. It appears that when Porter developed the model in the mid-1980s, the critical component of the external business environment was underappreciated. The external environment is of significant value when considering the full spectrum of the organizational production setting. Patterson (1995) emphasized the importance of supply chain management to the analysis of a company's product value because the movement of supplies and products into and out of an organization is critical to the success of the product.

The extended supply chain and the associated factors are examples of the external criticalities affecting business. For instance, the condition of the roadways used to move supplies into the manufacturing facility and product out to customers is a routine concern. Any impact on the

101

use of the roadways directly influences the timeline of product delivery. Another example is the ability of a critical component supplier to maintain the necessary level of supply to the company. Any disruptions in the logistical activities might result in complete product failure. Both examples are risk-management issues that affect the ability of the company to receive supplies or deliver a product to the market. Risk management is a necessary practice during organizational analysis. Failing to view the organization as a system and acknowledge the components is a serious problem.

Wurzer (1992) emphasized the critical value of newspaper agencies embracing alternate means of communicating the news such as a primary technology professional to promote the IT-oriented role of the news agency; and promoting the local interests of the community. Wurzer (1992) also indicated that embracing the need to grow organization revenue sources; providing a unique feature for the publication; use technology to promote the paper; and, increasing the capabilities of the technology-sponsored information databases are essential means of embracing alternatives.

SPECIFIC CHALLENGES FACING NEWSPAPERS

Sullivan (2012) emphasizes two factors are routinely discussed about the decline of traditional news media (e.g., newspapers), the loss of customers and advertising funds, and the increased reliance on the Internet for information. Social media may not promote the communication of actual news as a primary goal. However, there is a significant amount of information that is treated as news. The current election cycle for president possessed numerous accusations of false news stories. The treatment of social media as an outlet for factual news and not just opinion is a significant issue when looking at the problem of news communication.

Social media is an adjunct to existing technology. It provides an authoritative source of information for the users possessing a stake in the media source. For instance, during wars or disasters, social media outlets become primary sources of information about the events of the emergencies, and they become conduits for the victims to reach the outside world. The experiences from these examples have created a sense of value and importance with the information conveyed through the social media outlet. As a means to communicate the experiences of a phenomenon, there is value. However, as a means of communicating the actual news, there is a lack of validity associated with the information. Professional journalists have higher reputations and abilities to report a balanced story of an event; facts are verified and weak information discarded. Sullivan (2012) indicates a threat to democracy due to the proliferation of Internet sources and the decline of professional journalism. Wurzer (1992) indicated newspapers excel at documenting events and advertising (e.g., coupons and classified sections), and have a more personal relationship with the local customers (i.e., newspapers are delivered to homes like a service, and customers make a conscious decision to read the paper). The value of communicating factual news to the public is a long-standing attribute of a democratic society and facilitated through the trust of the newspaper or news outlet.

Younger audiences are frequent users of new forms of news communication such as social media (e.g., Facebook, Twitter, and Yelp), personal written and video blogs, and Internet news stories from sources of dubious credibility. People rely on the Internet for many forms of information and a sense of respectability through large numbers of followers; having large numbers of followers is not a reason to accept a source as credible – look at some of the train wreck celebrities that perpetuate false stories even though the false material has been debunked.

Lau and Wydick (2014) indicated that there are increased resources for new technology providing news outlets a more accessible opportunity to reach the public. However, there is also the degraded value of some news reporting because of the greater access to the world via technology (i.e., the greater the access to a broad audience, the more likely a story is poorly developed) and the opportunity for false news reporting (Lau and Wydick, 2014).

COMPETITIVE RECOMMENDATIONS

Newspapers still have an essential role in American society and a chance of survival (Pew Research Center, 2006). Facilitating a paradigm shift from desperation to success requires planning and understanding of the organizational dynamics. The newspaper industry should seek to embrace maximum efficiencies, seek diversification of outlets and new audiences, and promote the branding of excellence based on established journalistic tenets.

Ensure the organization is efficient and allows technology to create the most significant benefit. The alignment of organization functions with strategic goals is critical to success. Success requires that every business unit promotes the efficient interdependencies of a highly synergistically operating system. Learning new technology will likely become an inherent aspect of everyone's job. The acceptance of new technology by professional journalists is not an issue; journalists willingly seek new technology to improve the profession of journalism (Ekdale, Singer, Tully, & Harmsen, 2015). Mason (2014) emphasizes that new technology always comes along that results in process improvements; however, the requirement is the acceptance of the new technology.

Newspapers need to diversify and seek opportunities to reach new audiences. Relying on print as the only method of reaching the public is a foolish approach in the modern era of high technology. Online electronic versions of newspaper and powerful databases providing archived news editions are valuable to society. Perhaps increasing the partnerships or alliances that use a news outlet as a primary source of information will result in increased audiences. For instance, the Associated Press (AP) has been syndicated for years and appears in many newspapers. If a news agency promotes alliances like the AP approach, there is an opportunity to broaden the reach of the agency through multiple technical sources beyond the print format.

Maintain and enhance the branding of the newspaper as a source of quality journalism. The branding of news media as professionally developed and reported is one of the most important aspects of journalism. The fundamental credibility and reliability of reported news are the difference between a professionally balanced and factual story and an opinionated blog on the Internet. It is necessary to hire journalism professionals who are capable of performing multiple tasks connected with developing a multimedia approach to reaching new audiences while maintaining the image of excellence. Saltzis and Dickinson (2008) indicated that specially trained journalists that are adept at developing multimedia news articles (i.e., stories) are not widespread because of the complexity, added work to an already busy schedule, and concern for maintaining the required level of quality for journalism professionals. Nah, Yamamoto, Chung, and Zuercher (2015) emphasized the emergence of citizen reporters resulting in diverse community news content based on the value of local community amateurs augmenting the services of the newspaper. There is some logic in embracing quality community resources to promote partnerships between the community and the newspaper. Maintaining journalistic integrity and credibility are constant concerns whenever seeking to enhance the branding of an organization.

PERSONAL CHANGE MANAGEMENT

While the purpose of this book focuses on organizational change, organizations consist of people, and there are numerous self-help books aimed at personal change. The value of personal change from the perspective of this book is the inherent ability and willingness to maintain the flexibility of mind to change. There is comfort in maintaining the status quo, but change is inevitable and often required in many risk-oriented situations. Technology changes occur daily, requiring changes in protective measures and maintenance. If people are unwilling or unable to change to address the surrounding situations, the organization has failure built into the fabric of the culture.

Developing the ability to facilitate personal change is a desirable skill. It is the ability to accept the proper state of mind to acknowledge the fact that change happens. Leaders and managers plan for change to maintain the competitiveness of an organization. However, not everyone has that mindset of flexibility. Fostering the personal skill of change acceptance is both an organizational benefit and a personal development benefit. Leaders promote the vision necessary to maintain organizational competitiveness – that requires the ability to change. A wise employee will develop the ability to accept and seek out change as a professional development opportunity.

SUMMARY

The technological changes that occur in society influence not only the traditional concept of the print format of newspapers, but also the fundamental means of communicating information to society. The discussion addresses strategies promoting competition of the new industry. Technology is an ongoing example of societal change. Change impacts people in different degrees; some see it as a threat and others as an opportunity.

Moschella (2015) emphasized that to reach the 50% use level, the radio took 8 years (1922–1930), the telephone took 26 years (1920–1946), and the black and white television took 9 years (1939–1948). The modern technology devices are unstoppable change agents that continuously influence our lives at a quickening pace. The more modern technology devices such as the personal computer took 17 years (1976–1993); the use of the Internet took 9 years (1993–2002), and between 1980 and 1995, mobile phones took 15 years to achieve the 50% use level (Moschella, 2015).

The popularity and growth of companies such as Google, Facebook, and Amazon are not technological advancements, but instead, services that use applications already in use (Moschella, 2015). Moschella (2015) explains that technology advances are not accelerating but diversifying as into by-products of the existing technology foundations (e.g., home robots, smartwatches, and 3D consumer printers). The diversification of technological advances means more opportunities for users to acquire their respective desires (i.e., there are more means of communicating information between people). Diversification is an opportunity for newspapers to increase services and reach new audiences.

Jurevicius (2013) described Porter's VCA model as the identification and examination of the internal processes that lead to an understanding of the organizational functions that influence efficiencies and profits. The model consists of analyzing the dichotomy of primary (e.g., incoming supply chain; production; outgoing supply chain; marketing; customer service) and support functions (e.g., human resources; physical infrastructure; technology functions; strategic sourcing) within an organization (Jurevicius, 2013; Grant, 2016). Newspapers have a value chain that must be reviewed under a fresh perspective of modern technology, thereby facilitating new competitive approaches to success. Achieving success requires a plan to promote a fundamental paradigm shift from desperation to success. The newspaper industry should seek to embrace maximum efficiencies, seek diversification of outlets and new audiences, and promote the branding of excellence based on established journalistic tenets.

The value of personal change is the inherent ability and willingness to maintain the flexibility of mind to change. There is comfort in maintaining the status quo, but change is inevitable and often required in many risk-oriented situations. Technology changes occur daily, requiring changes in protective measures and maintenance. If people are unwilling or unable to change to address the surrounding situations, the organization has failure built into the fabric of the culture.

Developing the ability to facilitate personal change is a desirable skill. It is the ability to accept the proper state of mind to acknowledge the fact that change happens. Leaders and managers plan for change to maintain the competitiveness of an organization. However, not everyone has that mindset of flexibility. Fostering the personal skill of change acceptance is both an organizational benefit and a personal development benefit. Leaders promote the vision necessary to maintain organizational competitiveness – that requires the ability to change. A wise employee will develop the ability to accept and seek out change as a professional development opportunity.

REFERENCES

Curry, G. D., Leflar, J. J., Glasser, M., Grey, B., Jordan, T., Loyear, R., Ong, L., Preining, W., & Sobron, J. M. (2015). How social media is transforming crisis management and business continuity. *Journal of Physical Security*, 8(2), 15–36.

Ekdale, B., Singer, J. B., Tully, M., & Harmsen, S. (2015). Making change: Diffusion of technological, relational, and cultural innovation in the newsroom. *Journalism and Mass Communication Quarterly*, 92(4), 938–958.

Eriksson, C. I., Åkesson, M., & Lund, J. (2016). Designing ubiquitous media services - exploring the two-sided market of newspapers. *Journal of Theoretical and Applied Electronic Commerce Research*, 11(3), 1–19.

Grant, R. (2016). *Contemporary strategy analysis*. (9th ed.). Chichester, United Kingdom: Wiley.

Jurevicius, O. (2013, April). Value chain analysis. *Strategic Management Insight*. Retrieved from https://www.strategicmanagementinsight.com/tools/value-chain-analysis.html

Lau, M., & Wydick, B. (2014). Does new information technology lower media quality? The paradox of commercial public goods. *Journal of Industry, Competition and Trade*, 14(2), 145–157.

Mason, F. L. (2014, Dec 30). At the center of it all, part 3: Daily press embraces changing technology for changing industry. *TCA Regional News*.

Moschella, D. (2015, September). *The pace of technology change is not accelerating. [Leading Edge Forum: Monthly Research Commentary]*. Retrieved from https://d1xjoskxl9g04.cloudfront.net/media/assets/LEF_Research_Commentary_Pace_Of_Technology_Sept_2015.pdf

Nah, S., Yamamoto, M., Chung, D. S., & Zuercher, R. (2015). Modeling the adoption and use of citizen journalism by online newspapers. *Journalism and Mass Communication Quarterly*, 92(2), 399–420.

Patch, B. W. (1931). Radio competition with newspapers. *Editorial research reports 1931* (Vol. I). Washington, DC: CQ Press. Retrieved from http://library.cqpress.com/cqresearcher/cqresrre1931052100

Patterson, J. (1995). Adding value by managing supply chain activities. *Marketing News*, 29(15), 6.

Pew Research Center. (2006, July). *Challenges to the newspaper industry*. Retrieved from *Pew Research Center: Journalism & Media, Media & News* website: http://www.journalism.org/2006/07/24/challenges-to-the-newspaper-industry/

Saltzis, K., & Dickinson, R. (2008). Inside the changing newsroom: Journalists' responses to media convergence. *Aslib Proceedings*, 60(3), 216–228.

Sullivan, D. (2012). The changing business of journalism and its implications for democracy. *Journalism and Mass Communication Quarterly*, 89(1), 136–138.

Wurzer, H. K. (1992). The information explosion - A real opportunity for newspapers in the '90s. *Editor & Publisher*, 125(5), 2.

107

CHAPTER EXERCISES

1. **The Challenges of Implementing a Security Video System**
   Wendall is a security director with approval to install a new surveillance video system. He has focused on the technology and decided to implement an IP system using the organization's IT infrastructure as the backbone with dedicated switches. What are some of the critical communication issues that Wendall must address before moving too far into the planning process? What about privacy concerns?

2. **The Challenges of a Change Initiative**
   Consider your organization and the potential for developing a change initiative. What are the challenges that you expect to face? How will you overcome those challenges? Whom will you contact for assistance to facilitate support at different levels of the organization? What else will you have to consider to achieve success?

7

Final Thoughts

LIFELONG LEARNING

While the book is nearing the end, there is still a great deal of knowledge to obtain and process through practice and reflection for a novice change manager to become experienced. One of the most important lessons to learn from this book is that learning is not a "once and done" activity, but rather a lifelong journey. Please remember, as a change manager/project manager, you are trying to convince the organizational leadership to trust your abilities and knowledge concerning a project. Many experienced business unit leaders limit their learning opportunities because of the required effort and focus on learning new things – they rest on their laurels and begin to stagnate. Do not allow stagnation to creep into a promising career. Embrace the concept of lifelong learning and help to maintain a culture of change that is essential for an organization – lead by example. Organizations and people change on a routine basis, and that means the risk-oriented professional must continue to change and understand the reasons for a change.

The book has covered a considerable amount of material that will likely take time to process and place into the proper perspective of the respective organizations of the readership. That is expected and should provide opportunities to learn more about the concepts contained in this book. Organizations are complex systems and have multiple layers of meaning and nuance – things are not black and white, but various shades of gray. While this book contains a great deal of advice, please accept some additional advice on how to begin to use the material you have covered in this book.

ADVICE TO START A CHANGE INITIATIVE

Here are some suggestions to help you jump-start your new identity as a change manager.

- Begin slow and sure – apply the concepts learned in this book on small projects that are relatively uncomplicated.
- Apply Kotter's model (Kotter, 1996, 2012) as a framework and remember to continuously review and improve what is done as part of the project.
- Ensure that all communications are clear, honest, concise, but informative, and sincere; the audience will know the difference.
- Maintain communications throughout the project and work to keep people involved, even if they are not performing a function. Maintain the interest of those involved and help them to embrace the change initiative.
- Consider the significance of the cyclical and iterative nature of the PDCA (i.e., Plan-Do-Check-Act) approach referenced earlier in the text. Apply this approach to each of the eight steps of the Kotter model (Kotter, 1996, 2012). It is acceptable to go back and fix something that is not working right. Starting fresh might be necessary for that stage.
- Maintain the reporting and advisory connection with senior leadership. The senior leaders of an organization have a responsibility to both the organization and you as a developing employee. Allow them to help promote and maintain the change initiative.
- Learn from the simple project so that everyone is better prepared for the more complex projects. Learning should be fun, even when you get it wrong.
- Acknowledge mistakes and work to resolve any problems as a professional – do not try to hide a mistake. People often learn more from a mistake than from "getting it right." A mistake remains in a person's memory and helps them avoid making the same mistake. Reflecting on the mistake allows a person to apply the lesson to multiple situations and avoid making a mistake in numerous situations.
- Embrace the journey of lifelong learning. Consider how many things there are to learn and the opportunities that are presented following each session of learning. Have fun!

THE REMAINDER OF THE BOOK

The remainder of the book consists of appendices and references. The appendices contain valuable information to help each reader develop critical change management skills and perspectives. While there is a checklist for guiding the process of the change initiative, it is crucial to remember that change is a process. It is not a checklist activity. Without involving numerous people and embracing the concept of honest give-and-take and sharing ideas to develop a robust change initiative, the project will likely fail. Please remember an important point that was made earlier in the book – the change manager or project leader is not the most important person; the people in the organization are the most critical to a project. Make sure to involve them and build trust so that they will embrace the project.

REFERENCES

Kotter, J. P. (1996). Successful change and the force that drives it. *The Canadian Manager*, 21(3), 20–24.
Kotter, J. P. (2012). *Leading change*. Boston, MA: Harvard Business Review Press.

APPENDIX A

CHANGE MANAGEMENT PROJECT CHECKLIST

Project Name:
Business Unit:
Project Manager:
Deputy Project Manager:
Project Team Members:

Description of the Project:

CHANGE PROJECT CONSIDERATIONS

Justification of the Change Initiative
- Does the project align with established strategic goals?
- Have you promoted the business value of the project in terms of
  - business development,
  - goal achievement,
  - reputational value, and
  - other organizational benefits?
- Does the project have a project plan and schedule?
- Does the project have a risk management plan?
- Does the project have a change management plan?
- Does the project have a communications plan?

Support Involves Making Allies and Finding Champions
- Have you taken the time to learn about the organization and the groups?
- Have you identified a project champion at the senior management level?
- Have you presented the project as inclusive of membership?

- Have you identified allies?
- Have you identified resistors or sources of difficulty?
- Have you planned to keep everyone informed about the project?

Relate the Initiative to the Employees – Create Vested Interests
- Have you considered the marketing of the project?
- Have you indicated the value of the employees in developing and completing the project?
- Have you created a description of the project that resonates with the organizational culture?
- Are you using language that is appropriate for the organization? (hits the right tone)
- Have you identified connections (benefits) between the project and the employees?
- Have you met with groups and individuals to foster support for the project?
- Are you prepared to answer questions that could derail the project?
- Do you have answers to turn a project resistor into a project supporter?

Communication
- Have you developed a communications plan?
- Have you identified the audience(s) for your message(s)?
- Have you met with the leaders and significant group influencers?
- Do you understand the various groups (i.e., audience) involved in the project?
- Have you identified the issues that the employees see as valuable/ beneficial to gain their involvement?
- Have you identified the project resistors?
- Do you have responses to gain the support of the resistors?
- Have you identified your communication method to reach your audience(s)?
- Is the message simple?
- Is the message clear for the audience?
- Is the message genuine?
- Is the message personal and appealing to the audience?
- Is the message accurate honest?
- Does the message use plain, non-jargon language that everyone will understand?
- Is the message based on fact-based sources?
- Are you using examples (i.e., stories) to help create the initiative story at the company?

- Does the message ask for the support of the audience?
- Does the message indicate that the audience is the key to the project's success?
- Have you critiqued your message for items of interference?
- Have other people reviewed the message?
- Have you removed any ego-based references from the message?
- Do you think the audience understood your message?
- Are you avoiding long, information-packed email messages as a format to convey project details?
- Are you sharing the success of the project/program with those involved to facilitate an honest engagement?

Address Resistance to Change

- Do you understand that the workforce is critical to successful change?
- Do you understand that effective change is attributable to the employees, not the managers?
- Again, do you understand that the manager is not the critical component for success; the employees are the linchpin for success?
- Are you promoting the involvement of the employees in the development of the project?
- Are you fostering the creativity of the employees in developing the project?
- Are you seeking ideas (i.e., comments and feedback) from the employees?
- Do you recognize the achievements of the employees?
- Are you providing the resources, structure, and guidance throughout the change initiative?
- Are the employees actively participating in the change initiative?
- Do you recognize the business units for achieving project milestones?
- Do you recognize the feedback from employees to help improve the change initiative?
- Are you promoting the employees' involvement to show that they are essential to the success of the project/program?
- Are you sharing the credit for success with the employees and resistor elements?

Develop the Implementation Plan to Capture Regular Low-Hanging Fruit

- Have you developed a project plan?
- Have you identified project components that are achievable in the near-term?
- Is the implementation/project plan tied to the communication plan?

115

- Are you sending out messages to keep people informed and involved?
- Are you promoting the involvement of team members and the organizational teams?
- Have you developed awards or symbols of recognition for the teams and the individuals?
- Are you awarding the people and the teams involved?
- Have you created a friendly competition between the teams and the people?
- Are you reminding the people how the change initiative (i.e., the project) benefits them?
- Have you shown how the near-term/short-term wins benefit the people and the organization?
- Are you looking for ways to decrease the power of anyone to criticize the change negatively?
- Are you maintaining the morale of the participants?
- Are you trying to reenergize the change effort and maintain the overall momentum of the project?
- Do you have an established plan to communicate the project's accomplishments?
- Are you planning to achieve the project goals or just going through the project plan's motions?

Reinforce the Initiative with Regular Communications – Keep the Energy Going
- Are you maintaining a sense of urgency, and the flow of activities keeps the work progressing?
- Are you planning for the time when the project becomes a program?
- Are you maintaining the interpersonal relationships you have developed during the project?
- Are you looking long-term to maintain the value of the project goals?
- Are you prepared for the next stage of change initiative work?
- Are you maintaining communication with the project team (i.e., interested parties) and the organization?
- Are you producing quality management reports to facilitate your next project?

Establish the Change from a Project to a Program – Make it Part of the Organizational Culture
- Are you the manager of the new program?
- If not, has a manager been identified for the new program?

- Have you briefed the manager of the new program?
- Have you established the necessary framework for the project to become a viable program?
- Have you established a formal intranet site for the new program?
- Have you created the necessary internal team structure for the new program to operate within the host team?
- Have you established the new program within the management reporting structure?
- Have the business unit goals aligned with the strategic organizational goals?
- Have you noticed anything from the project that requires additional attention?
- Have you completed all of the project goals?
- Have you recognized the employees for their work and support?
- Have you developed a continuous improvement effort to maintain the quality of the new program?
- Have you learned from your experiences managing the project?
- Have you conducted a review of the project effort to help with the next project?

APPENDIX B

SCENARIO EXERCISE: PHYSICAL SECURITY SURVEILLANCE SYSTEM PROJECT

The change plan presented herein focuses on the implementation of a security video system in an organization. While the proposed change initiative plan is specific to a security video project, the plan is a template for a generic organization. The use of any template within an organization must undergo a careful review and probable revision because of the idiosyncrasies of the organization.

Each organization is unique to include the leaders, the managers, the subordinates, and the culture. Please do not think the template is acceptable without some degree of modification to fit the intended organization. The change plan is a good start, but it is only a start for the change manager to adjust according to the organization.

PROJECT SCENARIO

Tempo-Grande Corporation is a mid-sized professional services company providing consultants to financial, research, and defense contracts. The company is regulated through the federal government. There are approximately 1,479 employees in three main facilities in Maryland, Virginia, and Delaware. The company is about 8 years old and shows a healthy profit every year. The employees are well paid, well educated, and most maintain a federal security clearance for the various government contracts.

Senior leadership at Tempo-Grande decided to approve a security video system to increase the corporate security protective posture. The video coverage issue was identified through an audit of the facilities; as the government has increased the requirements contractors must comply with to obtain contracts; the company sees the security project as both a strategic competitive move and a compliance issue.

The video system is a new installation and identified as a digital network video recorder (server) using the buildings' IT infrastructure (e.g., cat 5E cabling, switches, routers, IDF, and data center rooms, and back-up battery protection). The project complied with the established IT protocols for the company.

Ed, the security director, is preparing to move the project forward. There were several meetings between Ed and the IT team assigned to the project to develop the initial project details for cost and scope to gain leadership approval. Ed wants to know how best to proceed with a change initiative plan.

CHANGE INITIATIVE PLAN – ISSUES TO CONSIDER

Justification for the Change Initiative

- The justification for the change initiative is more than just an order from leadership to get the project done. The project must have value to the organization so that the employees will understand the reasoning behind the change. For instance, enhancing the organization's security posture allows the business development team to bid on federal contracts requiring the planned upgrades.
- The change must be acceptable to the organizational culture to reduce the opportunity for significant resistance. Modern organizations often have close alignments between leadership and organizational culture resulting in the consistency of perspective. Resistance is still possible, but it must be considered as a potential problem throughout the change. The planned project allows the organization to increase business opportunities and keep the employees working. There is also a security consideration to protect the people and the property assets of the organization.
- Ensure there is a precise alignment between the change initiative and organizational goals. All project work must have an alignment to organizational goals to justify the project. However, there is value in promoting the alignment to lend credibility to the project – remember, marketing is critical.
- The example under discussion is one of video surveillance for physical security. Avoid claiming the justification for the project based on a security requirement. Align the project with a business requirement – there are no security requirements; there are only business requirements. Business leaders will respond better to the business alignment with the explanation of why the project is necessary. Several suggestions might serve for a new project.

- There are government regulations or contractual requirements to justify video surveillance;
  - Senior leadership's response to an incident to enhance the physical security of a facility(s) through video surveillance;
  - A risk assessment finding identifies the value for video surveillance of the facility(s) to decrease risk issues through an organizational treatment of risk;
- These examples support the project through the desire of the business leaders to conduct business – security is not the business. It is a means to support the business.

Author's Note: The installation of a surveillance system is a potential problem for the organization and the organizational culture. Unless the project is presented as a benefit to the employees, they may conclude that the video system is intended as a means to spy on the workers – a way to check when they arrive at work.

ESTABLISHING LEADERSHIP, MANAGEMENT, AND USER SUPPORT

- The establishment of the change team should reflect critical members from the top-down. The selection and identification of the leadership are critical to gaining the necessary senior-level support to include the leader-champion for the change initiative. The champion will support, defend, and go to war for the change – a true believer with the power to make a difference.
- The management of the change initiative depends on the selection of the right people to perform the actual project tasks – the managers make things happen. The managers help develop the change initiative project plans; this is where experienced project managers are of great value. While project managers are critical to the development of an efficient and effective project plan, a manager with an understanding of the dynamics of change management is crucial.
- Each organization will have an approach to the management of a project. Some have multiple managers performing separate functions that come together to produce the entire project. Some approaches will have a senior leader in charge of the project, with middle managers performing assigned tasks. Other approaches will have a middle

manager as the project leader coordinating with the appropriate contacts to complete the tasks.

- Consider using a recognized standard or governmental regulation to support the project. Using a conventional approach consisting of best practices (i.e., a standard or a regulation) establishes credibility and confidence in the project.

Author's Note: Gaining the right support for the installation of a surveillance system is critical to the success of the project. If possible, seek a believer in the project and not a senior leader in the chain of leadership that is forced to support the project. A proactive champion will help prevent problems from occurring.

ESTABLISHING A CONNECTION BETWEEN THE INITIATIVE AND THE EMPLOYEES

- It is critical to establish a connection between the change initiative and the employees. If the employees see the value of the change and establish a connection on a self-interested level, it will become much easier to implement the change.
- Look for the small connections that might lead to more substantial connections. Consider the essential aspects of work, life, and personal development as beginning points to make a connection between the employees and the change initiative. Remember, each person is different, and the connections might also reflect the same differences.

Author's Note: As noted above, the installation of a surveillance system is a potential problem for the organization and the organizational culture. Demonstrating the benefit and tangible value to the employees is one of the essential aspects of the project. It is not a waste of time or effort building a positive connection with the employees – they are the crux of success.

EFFECTIVE COMMUNICATION

- Effective communication is the most critical skill to possess in a long list of essential skills. The value of clear, concise language, both written and spoken, is critical to reaching an audience.

- Remember the necessary components of the communication dynamic (i.e., message sender, interference, and audience) and the goal of reducing the interference to enhance the chance the audience will understand the message. Some interference begins with the message because it is poorly written (i.e., poor grammar, poor word choice, unclear meaning, and weak conceptual foundation) or spoken. There is no value in using complicated language if it confuses people – concise sentences that are unfettered with jargon or highly technical words is the ideal approach.
- Learn about the members of the audience to ensure the proper level of language. Changing the message to match the audience is an excellent way to increase the reception of the message. A well-educated audience of technical experts or academicians will not balk at more advanced relevant language, but an audience of lay-people that does not possess the expertise of the topic is a different matter; keep it simple and direct.
- While language and format are essential to the audience receiving the message as intended, the intent and the interpersonal underpinnings of the message are often hidden issues that determine the outcome of the message. Audiences are in tune with the non-verbal aspects of the communicator. How the message is spoken is the unhidden complexity that communicators forget.
- The sincerity and honesty of the message is the crux of the issue. An audience will know if the speaker is insincere. Acknowledge mistakes that have been made and answer questions with honesty. It is better to say that an answer is unknown instead of trying to think of a quick response that is ill-formed.

Author's Note: Communication should be viewed as necessary throughout the entire video system project. Most projects will suffer from poor communication because there are insufficient messages or meetings, and the information is not presented at the right level of focus.

MANAGING RESISTANCE TO CHANGE

- Resistance to change is a deep-seated complex issue that should be addressed at the beginning of the project. Resistance is not always about the project. You must understand the organization and the operational issues impacting the business. Make sure to select the right time to suggest the project – think both tactically and strategically.

- Consider the types of resistance associated with the project. Employees might be cynical of the project because they have seen other projects that have failed or did not live up to the promoted expectations. Some employees might distrust the organization's leaders because of labor issues or perceived problems with pay and benefits. The leaders might doubt the project and offer resistance because it is safer to resist the project than to take a chance on the project failing or changing a dynamic that is beneficial to the leader.

- The empowerment of the workforce is critical to successful change. Promote involvement, creativity, seek ideas (i.e., comments and feedback) from the employees, and recognize achievements. Develop the "vested interest" concept of building support for the project.

- Effective change is attributable to the employees, not the managers. Managers provide the resources, structure, and guidance throughout the change initiative. However, the employees must willingly participate in the change to see success.

- Recognize the feedback from employees that help improve the change initiative. Feedback is a great way to build the involvement of employees and show that they are essential to the success of the project/program. The manager should spread the credit for success – the manager is not the key component for success; the employees are the linchpin for success.

Author's Note: While considering the root causes for resistance to change, consider how to work with those resisting. A project involving the use of the IT backbone of the organization may create concerns for IT professionals. Work with them to resolve issues before they become problems. Identify the existing IT protocols for cabling, switch management, security measures, and work with the owners of the IT network so that minor issues never become problems. Creating a partnership of equals allows for the building of trust that will pay dividends in the current project and future projects.

PRACTICAL PLANS

- Organizational projects require various plans to gain support and approval to proceed. Plans allow the organizers to demonstrate the organization of the project – plans are critical to the success of the project.
- Make sure to use the existing organizational project structure and approaches. Using existing approaches will allow the leaders to understand and feel more comfortable with the project. While the project might be innovative and transformational, try to use a known means to achieve the project goals.
- Plans based on reliable project management approaches (e.g., the Project Management Institute Body of Knowledge Standard) are the best ways to achieve project goals. Projects must have established management structures of performance and authority, clear objectives, established and available resources, an approved budget that is reasonable, a communication plan that is associated with the change management plan, and a thorough project plan.
- Selecting the right people for the project is critical to success. The people in the organization will determine the success of the change (i.e., the project), and they should be representative of the teams involved in the change.
- It is also wise to consider the risks associated with the project. Identifying the risks at the beginning of the project will allow the team to address and mitigate the risks early in the planning process.

Author's Note: A video surveillance system has numerous complex issues to address early in the planning stage. For instance, if a PTZ camera is receiving power from the network, it is vital to verify that the power is sufficient to control and hold the programming of the camera. Local power for remote cameras might be necessary. Work with the project team to identify and resolve potential issues. The facilities management team could offer considerable assistance with power discussions – develop a team and allow them to become involved in a practical and meaningful way.

MOMENTUM THROUGH COMMUNICATION

- Communication is the most critical aspect of any project because everything is dependent upon effective communication. It is necessary to develop a good communication plan that augments the change management plan.
- Maintaining a sense of urgency and flow of activities keeps the work progressing. Maintaining the momentum of the project is essential to avoid stoppages or people losing interest in the project – plan for the continuation of the initiative and the reenergizing of the people and the activities.
- Keep a steady flow of energy going into the initiative so that the activities maintain forward momentum.
- Ensure to establish and maintain regular updates to management and the organization. The promotion of the project through organizational updates reminds people that the project is managed and conducted by professionals. It is necessary to keep the change initiative in organizational awareness.
- It is wise to have a communication strategy that is grounded in a marketing perspective.

Author's Note: Consider developing a multimedia approach to communicating information. Video surveillance systems are typically private and protected to avoid breaching privacy concerns. While the employees need to understand that the security department will maintain that privacy, some examples can be provided to help educate the employees on the capabilities of the system. For instance, work with the equipment installer to obtain demonstrations of the power of the cameras to capture people in the parking lot, pretending to vandalize cars. Show the resolution capabilities of the camera from several distances. Make sure to express the purpose of the video system and how it protects the people and the property associated with the organization. It is also an excellent opportunity to correct some of the fallacies generated from television and the cinema concerning video systems.

INSTITUTIONALIZATION OF THE INITIATIVE

- When the project is completed, there is often an expectation that the maintenance of the program is necessary to keep the work progressing.
- Regular management reports on the program and periodic updates to the organization on the critical value that is generated by the program is necessary to remind people that the change initiative produced tangible results benefiting the organization.
- A useful way to view the change process is a cycle of movement from planning through evaluation with iterative change and continuous improvement as the constants.

Author's Note: IT technology is an ever-changing product that must remain current to continue to provide the promoted value. Make sure that leadership understands before the project begins that a maintenance program is essential to the success of the system. Once the system is operational, everyone will have an expectation of the capabilities of the system. Hopefully, those expectations are grounded in reality. Make sure that people understand the actual capabilities of the video system before the system goes live. Future projects will depend on the success of the current project.

APPENDIX C

SCENARIO EXERCISE: BUSINESS CONTINUITY PROGRAM DEVELOPMENT PROJECT

The change plan presented herein focuses on the implementation of a business continuity program in an organization. While the proposed change initiative plan is specific to a business continuity program project, the plan is a template for a generic organization. The use of any template within an organization must undergo a careful review and probable revision because of the idiosyncrasies of the organization.

Each organization is unique to include the leaders, the managers, and the culture. Please do not think the template is acceptable without some degree of modification to fit the intended organization. The change plan is a good start, but it is only a start for the change manager to adjust according to the organization.

PROJECT SCENARIO

Tempo-Grande Corporation is a mid-sized professional services company providing consultants to financial, research, and defense contracts. The company is regulated through the federal government. There are approximately 1,479 employees in three main facilities in Maryland, Virginia, and Delaware. The company is about eight years old and shows a healthy profit every year. The employees are well paid, well educated, and most maintain a federal security clearance for the various government contracts.

Senior leadership at Tempo-Grande decided to seek specific federal contracts that require conformance with ISO 22301:2019 (i.e., business continuity management system) to gain certification indicating compliance with the standard. The senior leaders had discussed implementing a BC Program to enhance the continuity of the organization due to an increase in risk issues. The certification from a third-party auditor confirming conformance with the ISO 22301:2019 standard is necessary to bid on specific federal contracts; the contracts would bring in profitable business for the organization. The company sees the development of a BC Program as both a strategic competitive move and an ethical business compliance issue.

The talent management team posted for two initial business continuity (BC) positions. The BC positions consisted of a manager and a specialist with required certifications in business continuity. The positions were filled with experienced and well-trained professionals. The manager conveyed concern about the limited staff of the BC team and the planned conformance with ISO 22301:2019. While the standard consists of best practices developed through a broad-based industry neutral team of developers, conformance is challenging and resource-intensive.

Conforming to ISO 22301:2019 is time-consuming and work-intensive. The decision to proceed should be based on business needs. Does the cost in resources justify the benefit derived from conformance to the standard? That decision has already been made for the scenario. However, in reality, the project is lengthy, and a small team should expect to take several years to conform to the standard. The BC manager begins developing plans to establish the BC program and the ISO 22301:2019 conformance project.

CHANGE INITIATIVE PLAN – ISSUES TO CONSIDER

Justification for the Change Initiative

- The justification for the change initiative is more than just an order from leadership to get the project done. The project must have value to the organization so the employees will understand the reasoning behind the change. For instance, enhancing the continuity posture of the organization allows the business development team to bid on federal contracts requiring conformance to a particular standard.
- The change must be acceptable to the organizational culture to reduce the opportunity for significant resistance. Modern organizations often have close alignments between leadership and organizational culture resulting in the consistency of perspective. Resistance is still possible, but it must be considered as a potential problem throughout the change. The planned project allows the organization to increase business opportunities and keep the employees working. Enhancing the business continuity measures of an organization allows for the protection of the people and the property assets of the organization.

- Ensure there is a precise alignment between the change initiative and organizational goals. All project work must have an alignment to organizational goals to justify the project. However, there is value in promoting the alignment to lend credibility to the project – remember, marketing is critical.
- The example under discussion is one of implementing the ISO 22301:2019 standard for business continuity. Avoid claiming the justification for the project is based on an organizational requirement. Align the project with a business requirement – there are no business continuity requirements; there are only business requirements. Business leaders will respond better to the business alignment with the explanation of why the project is necessary. Several suggestions might serve for a new project.
  - There are government regulations or contractual requirements to justify conforming to ISO 22301:2019.
  - Senior leadership's response to an incident (e.g., a hurricane or a power outage) to enhance the business continuity of a business unit or team.
  - A risk assessment finding identifies the value for enhancing business continuity conformance to best practices (i.e., ISO 22301:2019) to decrease risk issues through an organizational treatment of risk.
  - These examples support the project through the desire of the business leaders to conduct business – business continuity is not the business. It is a means to support the business.

Author's Note: It should be easy to establish a justification for conforming to ISO 22301:2019 as long as the logical basis is business-related. The above information should help establish proper project scope and purpose but remember to indicate linkages between conformance and the success of the organization.

ESTABLISHING LEADERSHIP, MANAGEMENT, AND USER SUPPORT

- The establishment of the change team should reflect critical members from the top down. The selection and identification of the leadership are critical to gaining the necessary senior-level support to include the leader-champion for the change initiative. The champion will support, defend, and go to war for the change – a true believer with the power to make a difference.

- The management of the change initiative depends on the selection of the right people to perform the actual project tasks – the managers make things happen. The managers help develop the change initiative project plans; this is where experienced project managers are of great value. While project managers are critical to the development of an efficient and effective project plan, a manager with an understanding of the dynamics of change management is crucial.
- Each organization will have an approach to the management of a project. Some have multiple managers performing separate functions that come together to produce the entire project. Some approaches will have a senior leader in charge of the project, with middle managers performing assigned tasks. Other approaches will have a middle manager as the project leader coordinating with the appropriate contacts to complete the tasks.
- Consider using a recognized standard or governmental regulation to support the project. Using a conventional approach consisting of best practices (i.e., a standard or a regulation) establishes credibility and confidence in the project.

Author's Note: Since the ISO 22301:2019 project is complicated and resource-intensive, it is critical to gain the right support for the success of the project. Multiple tasks require the involvement of senior leadership to develop the necessary foundation for the project. If possible, seek a believer in the project and not a senior leader in the chain of leadership that is forced to support the project. A proactive champion will help prevent problems from occurring.

ESTABLISHING A CONNECTION BETWEEN THE INITIATIVE AND THE EMPLOYEES

- It is critical to establish a connection between the change initiative and the employees. If the employees see the value of the change and establish a connection on a self-interested level, it will become much easier to implement the change.
- Look for the small connections that might lead to more substantial connections. Consider the essential aspects of work, life, and personal

development as beginning points to make a connection between the employees and the change initiative. Remember, each person is different, and the connections might also reflect the same differences.

Author's Note: It is imperative to establish a connection between the value of the business continuity project and program and the employees so that they embrace the potential for the organization and the organizational culture. Demonstrating the benefit and tangible value to the employees is one of the essential aspects of the project. It is not a waste of time or effort building a positive connection with the employees – they are the crux of success.

EFFECTIVE COMMUNICATION

- Effective communication is the most critical skill to possess in a long list of essential skills. The value of clear, concise language, both written and spoken, is critical to reaching an audience.
- Remember the necessary components of the communication dynamic (i.e., message sender, interference, and audience) and the goal of reducing the interference to enhance the chance the audience will understand the message. Some interference begins with the message because it is poorly written (i.e., poor grammar, poor word choice, unclear meaning, and weak conceptual foundation) or spoken. There is no value in using complicated language if it confuses people – concise sentences that are unfettered with jargon or highly technical words is the ideal approach.
- Learn about the members of the audience to ensure the proper level of language. Changing the message to match the audience is an excellent way to increase the reception of the message. A well-educated audience of technical experts or academicians will not balk at more advanced relevant language, but an audience of lay-people that does not possess the expertise of the topic is a different matter; keep it simple and direct.
- While language and format are essential to the audience receiving the message as intended, the intent and the interpersonal underpinnings of the message are often hidden issues that determine the outcome of the message. Audiences are in tune with the non-verbal aspects of the communicator. How the message is spoken is the unhidden complexity that communicators forget.

- The sincerity and honesty of the message is the crux of the issue. An audience will know if the speaker is insincere. Acknowledge mistakes that have been made and answer questions with honesty. It is better to say that an answer is unknown instead of trying to think of a quick response that is ill-formed.

Author's Note: Communication should be viewed as necessary throughout the entire business continuity project. Most projects will suffer from poor communication because there are insufficient messages or meetings, and the information is not presented at the right level of focus. It is advisable to use a variety of methods to communicate vital messages to the organization. Remember, modern organizations consist of employees from baby boomers to generations X, Y, Z, and millennials; each group prefers a different method of communication. Some will like handouts, some will like electronic messages (e.g., email or videos), and some will prefer instant messaging formats (i.e., tweets) to learn about a project.

MANAGING RESISTANCE TO CHANGE

- Resistance to change is a deep-seated complex issue that should be addressed at the beginning of the project. Resistance is not always about the project. You must understand the organization and the operational issues impacting the business. Make sure to select the right time to suggest the project – think both tactically and strategically.
- Consider the types of resistance associated with the project. Employees might be cynical of the project because they have seen other projects that have failed or did not live up to the promoted expectations. Some employees might distrust the organization's leaders because of labor issues or perceived problems with pay and benefits. The leaders might doubt the project and offer resistance because it is safer to resist the project than to take a chance on the project failing or changing a dynamic that is beneficial to the leader.
- The empowerment of the workforce is critical to successful change. Promote involvement, creativity, seek ideas (i.e., comments and feedback) from the employees, and recognize achievements. Develop the "vested interest" concept of building support for the project.
- Effective change is attributable to the employees, not the managers. Managers provide the resources, structure, and guidance throughout

the change initiative. However, the employees must willingly participate in the change to see success.

- Recognize the feedback from employees that help improve the change initiative. Feedback is a great way to build the involvement of employees and show that they are essential to the success of the project/program. The manager should spread the credit for success – the manager is not the key component for success; the employees are the linchpin for success.

Author's Note: As discussed earlier, consider the root causes for resistance to change, and consider how to work with those employees resisting the change project. Many people will indicate that they are too busy to become involved in conducting BIAs. Ensuring that all of the early steps of establishing the justifications and approvals for the project will help reduce some of the resistance. It is a requirement of ISO 22301:2019 that a business continuity policy exists for the organization. Ensure that the policy is developed and published before trying to implement other aspects of the project that require employee involvement. Creating a partnership of equals allows for the building of trust that will pay dividends in the current project and future projects.

PRACTICAL PLANS

- Organizational projects require various plans to gain support and approval to proceed. Plans allow the organizers to demonstrate the organization of the project – plans are critical to the success of the project.
- Make sure to use the existing organizational project structure and approaches. Using existing approaches will allow the leaders to understand and feel more comfortable with the project. While the project might be innovative and transformational, try to use a known means to achieve the project goals.
- Plans based on reliable project management approaches (e.g., the Project Management Institute Body of Knowledge Standard) are the best ways to achieve project goals. Projects must have established management structures of performance and authority, clear objectives, established and available resources, an approved budget that is reasonable, a communication plan that is associated with the change management plan, and a thorough project plan.

- Selecting the right people for the project is critical to success. The people in the organization will determine the success of the change (i.e., the project), and they should be representative of the teams involved in the change.
- It is also wise to consider the risks associated with the project. Identifying the risks at the beginning of the project will allow the team to address and mitigate the risks early in the planning process.

Author's Note: Initiating a change to conform to ISO 22301:2019 requires several plans (i.e., think approaches if plans are undesirable) to ensure success. Approach the plans from a straightforward perspective following everything presented in this book. For instance, document the communication plan and list each of the elements/vital methods necessary to reach the organization and communicate the critical messages. Keeping things simple will help reduce the stress involved in the project.

MOMENTUM THROUGH COMMUNICATION

- Communication is the most critical aspect of any project because everything is dependent upon effective communications. It is necessary to develop a good communication plan that augments the change management plan.
- Maintaining a sense of urgency and flow of activities keeps the work progressing. Maintaining the momentum of the project is essential to avoid stoppages or people losing interest in the project – plan for the continuation of the initiative and the reenergizing of the people and the activities.
- Keep a steady flow of energy going into the initiative so that the activities maintain forward momentum.
- Ensure to establish and maintain regular updates to management and the organization. The promotion of the project through organizational updates reminds people that the project is managed and conducted by professionals. It is necessary to keep the change initiative in organizational awareness.
- It is wise to have a communication strategy that is grounded in a marketing perspective.

Author's Note: Consider developing a multimedia approach to communicating information. Planning and implementing ISO 22301:2019 requires considerable effort and involvement from the organization. Conducting the business impact analyses (BIA) throughout the organization or that portion of the organization that falls within the scope is time-consuming. The approach taken to conduct the BIAs will determine the amount of time. For instance, using a manual approach such as Word or Excel files will likely increase the time by a factor of four. An electronic tool will decrease time, but there is a learning curve to benefit from the tool. Demonstrate the power of the electronic approach and the internal metrics that are undoubtedly part of the application. If a manual approach is used, demonstrate the simplicity and cost savings; try to downplay the amount of time required.

INSTITUTIONALIZATION OF THE INITIATIVE

- When the project is completed, there is often an expectation that the maintenance of the program is necessary to keep the work progressing.
- Regular management reports on the program and periodic updates to the organization on the critical value that is generated by the program is necessary to remind people that the change initiative produced tangible results benefiting the organization.
- A useful way to view the change process is a cycle of movement from planning through evaluation with iterative change and continuous improvement as the constants.

When attempting to conform to ISO 22301:2019, it is advisable to conduct a gap(s) analysis of the organization compared to the requirements of the standard. Figure C.1 is a partial gaps analysis of clause 4 of ISO 22301:2019. It is presented as an example of how to document a gap analysis. As stated earlier, the change initiative manager should use the project management approaches used by the organization. Using established tools and approaches will resonate with senior leaders and build confidence in the project and the leadership. While implementing ISO 22301:2019 requires many plans and documents demonstrating how the standard requirements are in operation, the organization

Clause	Requirements	Conform to the Requirements of ISO 22310:2019 (Yes or No)	Author Contributed Practical Implementation Issues
4	**Contextual Understanding of the Organization**		
4.1	**Understanding the Organization and its Context**		
	The organization shall determine external and internal issues that are relevant to its purpose and that affect its ability to achieve the intended outcome(s) of its BCMS.		The practical implementation of ISO 22301 must rest upon a firm foundation of understanding the organizational goals of the BC management program. It is necessary to understand the scope of the BC program as well as the internal and external environments in which the organization operates. Once you know the anticipated outcomes of the BC program and the various internal and external issues impacting the organizational BC program, it is critical to identify the interested parties associated with the organization. The interested parties (this reference replaced stakeholders) have different priorities and goal expectations, their expectations should be part of the BC discussion to ensure as varied a project scope as feasible - remember that it is important to generate vested interest in the change initiative.
4.2	**Understanding the Needs and Expectations of Interested Parties**		ISO changed the use of stakeholder(s) to interested parties in their standards to reflect the broad-based nature of people interested and having social, financial, organizational, and other forms of vested interest in an organization. There are varied perspectives of interest in the implementation of a standard and the potential outcomes. Remember, modern organizations are complex systems consisting of internal and external dependencies. For instance, a consulting organization might benefit from conforming to ISO 2230:2019 because of federal bidding considerations. Third party relationships often involve demonstrating the business continuity and disaster recovery capabilities of the parties involved.
4.2.1	General		
	When establishing its BCMS, the organization shall determine:		
a)	the interested parties that are relevant to the BCMS;		Consider all of the interested parties to include organizations.
b)	the relevant requirements of these interested parties.		Consider the relevant requirements of all the interested parties.

Figure C.1 Gap Analysis Considerations – Partial List (the clause requirements were quoted from ISO 22301:2019).

	0	Task Mode	WBS	Task Name	% Complete	Duration	Start	Finish	Resource Names
1	✓	⭐	1	⊿ CY2019	100%	90 days	Tue 9/3/19	Mon 1/6/20	
2	✓	⭐	1.1	⊿ Q4	100%	90 days	Tue 9/3/19	Mon 1/6/20	
3	✓	⭐	1.1.1	Develop Project Team and the Initial Plans of the Project	100%	90 days	Tue 9/3/19	Mon 1/6/20	Project Team
4		⭐	2	⊿ CY2020	24%	62 days	Mon 1/6/20	Tue 3/31/20	
5		⭐	2.1	⊿ Q1	85%	62 days	Mon 1/6/20	Tue 3/31/20	
6		⭐	2.1.1	Create the Communication Plan for the Project	25%	20 days	Mon 1/6/20	Fri 1/31/20	Project Team
7		⭐	2.1.2	Draft and Publish BC Policy	45%	62 days	Mon 1/6/20	Tue 3/31/20	Project Team
8		⭐	2.1.3	Complete Change Management Plan	60%	40 days	Mon 1/6/20	Fri 2/28/20	Project Team
9		⭐	2.1.4	Conduct and Complete Gap Analysis	85%	62 days	Mon 1/6/20	Tue 3/31/20	Project Team
10		⭐	2.1.5	Meet With the Impacted Business Teams	10%	62 days	Mon 1/6/20	Tue 3/31/20	Project Team

Figure C.2 Project Plan Example – Partial List.

might have project-oriented documentation that is appropriate. Here is a list of suggested plans for the project:

- Project Management Plan
- Change Management Plan
- Communication Plan
- Risk Management Plan
- Resources Plan (e.g., people, budget, equipment, locations)
- Include other organization-specific documents required for major projects

The examples in Figures C.1 and C.2 are presented to illustrate the types of documents that are helpful in planning and implementing a business continuity change initiative. These figures are partial examples and do not list all of the items necessary for the gap analysis or the project plan. The development of the project plan is complex and requires a degree of experience. Requesting a project manager from the organization will facilitate the management of the project and bring a high degree of competency to developing the plan.

Author's Note: Conforming to ISO 22301:2019 is sophisticated and extremely resource-intensive. It is beneficial and necessary to develop the implementation plans of the project to ensure that the conformance is long-lasting. The standard is intended for a program and not a project. The project will require considerable organizational resources to achieve conformance. Once conformance is achieved, it is wasteful to allow the management system to degrade (i.e., become a nonconformity). It is incumbent upon the project manager to demonstrate the absolute need to maintain conformity through a robust business continuity program.

APPENDIX D

SUGGESTED FURTHER RESEARCH AND READINGS

The citations used in this book are valuable resources for adding to your knowledge. The following suggested resources are intended as specific additions to consider for those risk-oriented professionals looking for more information about several of the topics covered in the book. A professional that is serious about life-long learning commits time and resources to regular learning activities. Reading is one of the best learning activities available to a professional.

PROFESSIONAL ORGANIZATIONS

Author's Note: I maintain the highest certifications from ASIS International and Disaster Recovery Institute International, and I am a firm supporter of their value to industry professionals. While I do not have professional certifications through the other organizations listed, I support their value to our change management community.

ASIS International

ASIS International is a global community of security practitioners. ASIS offers educational programs, thought leadership in a variety of risk-oriented topics, and professional certifications focusing on security management, physical security, and investigations. ASIS is also known for developing many ANSI-approved standards on organizational resilience, risk, business continuity, and numerous security-related topics. Anyone interested in security should visit the ASIS homepage and consider membership. The home page for ASIS can be found at https://www.asisonline.org/

Association of Change Management Professionals

The Association of Change Management Professionals (ACMP) is an organization dedicated to promoting change management practices for broad-based organizational professionals. The home page for ACMP can be found at https://www.acmpglobal.org/

Disaster Recovery Institute International

Disaster Recovery Institute International (DRI International) is the largest nonprofit organization focusing on business continuity, disaster recovery, cyber resilience, and other related topics through education programs and certifications. DRI International is a thought leader in the overarching fields of business continuity and disaster recovery. DRI is a highly respected organization; the professional practices document is an excellent resource for anyone involved in business continuity. The home page for DRI can be found at https://drii.org/

Project Management Institute

The Project Management Institute (PMI) is the premier organization for information about project management practices. PMI maintains a valuable source of project knowledge; the Project Management Body of Knowledge is a must-have for anyone involved in project management. The home page for PMI can be found at https://www.pmi.org/

CHANGE MANAGEMENT REFERENCES

Busby, N. (2017). *The shape of change: A guide to planning, implementing and embedding organizational change*. New York, NY: Routledge.

Coughlan, D. & Rashford, N. (2006). *Organizational change and strategy: An interlevel dynamics approach*. New York, NY: Routledge.

Hayes, J. (2014). *The theory and practice of change management* (4th ed.). New York, NY: Palgrave Macmillan.

Hollman, P., Devane, T., & Cady, S. (Eds.). (2007). *The change handbook: The definitive resource on today's best methods for engaging whole systems* (2nd ed.). San Francisco, CA: Berrett Koehler.

Kotter, J. P. (2012). *Leading change*. Boston, MA: Harvard Business Review Press.

Senge, P. (2006). *The fifth discipline: The art and practice of the learning organization*. New York, NY: Doubleday.

INDEX

Page numbers in *italic* indicate figures. Page numbers in **bold** indicate tables.

Printed in the United States
by Baker & Taylor Publisher Services